INHERIT THE ATCHAFALAYA

Greg Guirard

Clay Damien

Just after sunrise in a thick grove of second-growth bald cypress trees near Bayou Benoit.

INHERIT THE ATCHAFALAYA

Greg Guirard

C. Ray Brassieur

Center for Louisiana Studies
University of Louisiana at Lafayette
2007

Published by the Center for Louisiana Studies
PO Box 40831
Lafayette, LA 70504-0831

Library of Congress Cataloging-in-Publication Data

Guirard, Greg, 1937-
Inherit the Atchafalaya / Greg Guirard, C. Ray Brassieur.
p. cm.

ISBN 1-887366-76-8 (alk. paper)

1. Atchafalaya River Watershed (La.)--History. 2. Human ecology--Louisiana--Atchafalaya River Watershed. 3. Swamp ecology--Louisiana--Atchafalaya River Watershed. 4. Boats and boating--Louisiana--Atchafalaya River Watershed. 5. Atchafalaya River Watershed (La.)--Pictorial works. 6. Atchafalaya River Watershed (La.)--Environmental conditions.
I. Brassieur, C. Ray. II. University of Louisiana at Lafayette. Center for Louisiana Studies. III. Title.

F377.A78G83 2007

508.763--dc22   2007007909

Published in collaboration with the Louisiana Department of Natural Resources.

CONTENTS

Lifelong residents of the Atchafalaya Basin, Harold and Myrtle Bigler at their favorite sitting spot, an overturned wooden fishing hull next to their home on the main channel of the Atchafalaya River.

Atchafalaya
River Basin

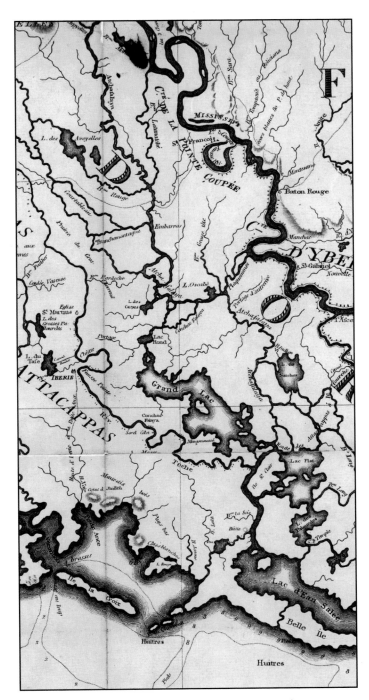

Atchafalaya region of Louisiana, 1806.
(From map by Barthéleme Lafon.)

Time Line of Important Events
Related to the Atchafalaya Basin

1800 – 1838

Atchafalaya is but a bayou; water slowly seeps beneath a thirty-plus mile obstruction of logs and debris known as the "raft."

1839 – 1850

Substantial portion of the "raft" is removed from the upper Atchafalaya, dramatically increasing the flow of water downriver. With navigation between the Red, Atchafalaya, and Mississippi rivers possible, the lower Mississippi Valley and the Atchafalaya Basin begin to develop commercially from agriculture, forestry, fishing, trapping, and other, smaller industries, such as moss collection. Floods become more severe during this period.

1850

The United States Congress passes the Swamp and Overflow Land Act, permitting the federal government to deed millions of acres of swampland to states along rivers; and allowing states to then sell off the swampland to pay for various flood control activities, including construction of a few low levees. The Act is usually viewed as providing the foundation for the devastation of the great cypress swamp forest.

1850 – 1860

With floods growing more severe each year, farmland under cultivation in the Basin begins to fail. During the second half of the nineteenth century, the wetland environment of the Basin greatly expands, marking the "birth" of this magnificent floodplain.

One of the most severe floods to date results in the Atchafalaya drawing in more water from both the Red and Mississippi rivers, causing a dramatic increase in the width and depth of the maturing river.	1863
Old growth cypress is logged to virtual extinction in the Basin with significant portions of the swamp being clearcut.	1870s – 1930s
Most severe flood of the nineteenth century.	1882

~ GOLDEN ERA OF ATCHAFALAYA SWAMP LIFE ~

The worst flood on record in the Lower Mississippi Valley destroys property and takes lives from Cairo, Illinois to the Gulf of Mexico.	1927
The Flood Control Act of 1928 transforms the Atchafalaya Basin into a "Spillway."	1928
Annual springtime flooding gradually leads to the abandonment of all settlements within the Atchafalaya, including Atchafalaya Station, Pelba, and Bayou Chene by 1952.	1928 – 1952
Old River Control Structure goes into operation with the goal of regulating the flow of water into the Atchafalaya from the Red and Mississippi rivers.	1963
First Atchafalaya Basin Commission is formed by Governor John McKeithen.	1970

Red River Raft, mid-nineteenth century.

Bird's eye view of Atchafalaya Station in 1940. (Courtesy of the State Library of Louisiana.)

The three inlets of the Old River Control Complex, looking south. The Mississippi River is to the left and can be seen winding through the top of the image; the Atchafalaya system is to the right.

U.S. Interstate-10 elevated expressway over the Atchafalaya Basin.

1972	The Attakapas Wildlife Management Area is created from 27,962 acres of land accumulated at a site which was formerly Grand Lake.
1973	At the height of a huge spring flood, one of the guide walls of the Old River Control Structure completely fails, putting the entire structure in danger of collapse. At the height of the flood, more than a third of the flow of the Mississippi goes down the Atchafalaya; had the structure toppled, the Atchafalaya more than likely would have succeeded in its quest to steal Old Man River. Interstate-10 elevated expressway over the Atchafalaya Basin is completed.
1981	The Dow Corporation announces its donation of 30,000 acres of land within the Basin to the state of Louisiana. Accessibility and usage of private, public, and governmental lands become increasingly contested issues.
1983	Annual springtime floods are the highest in recent memory, resulting in one of the last really good commercial fishing seasons within the Atchafalaya Basin; smaller floods in 1993, 1995, and 1997 also benefit fishermen.
1985	Public Law 99-88 by Congress enacts the Multipurpose Plan presented by the U.S. Army Corps of Engineers, which authorizes $250 million to preserve and restore the Basin ecosystem where possible.
1999	Act 920 of the Louisiana Legislature authorizes the State Master Plan for the Atchafalaya Basin Program with a budget of $85 million over fifteen years and specifically addresses access, easements, water management, and recreation.
2004	Atchafalaya Welcome Center opens at Butte LaRose.

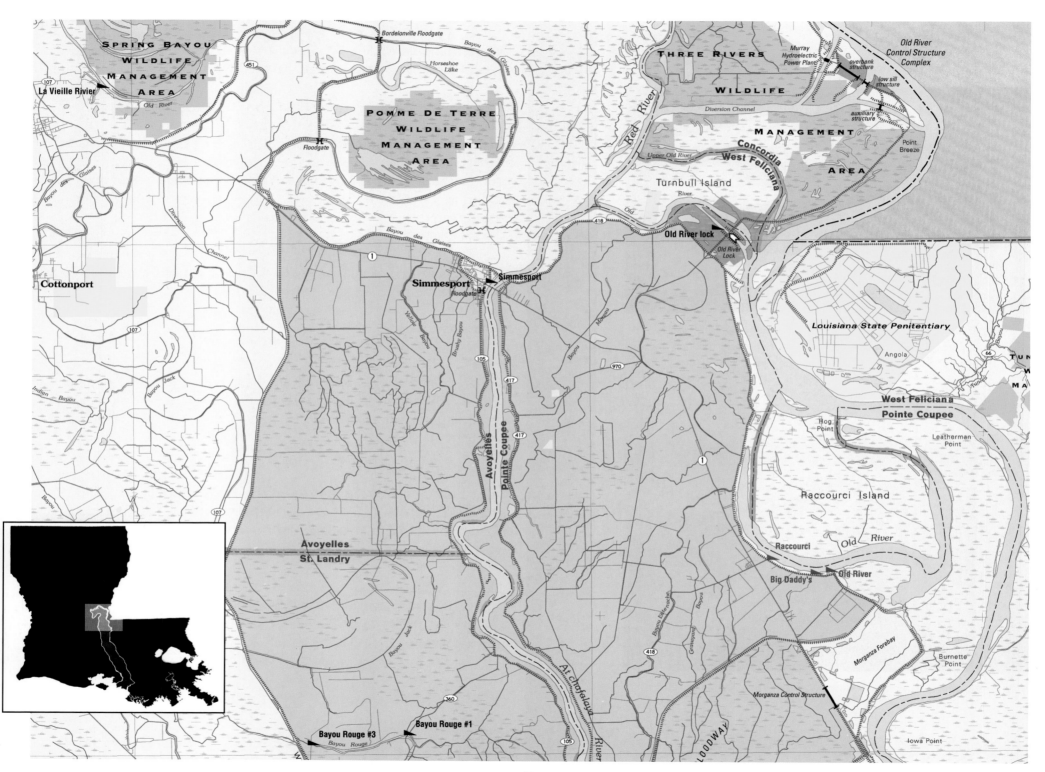

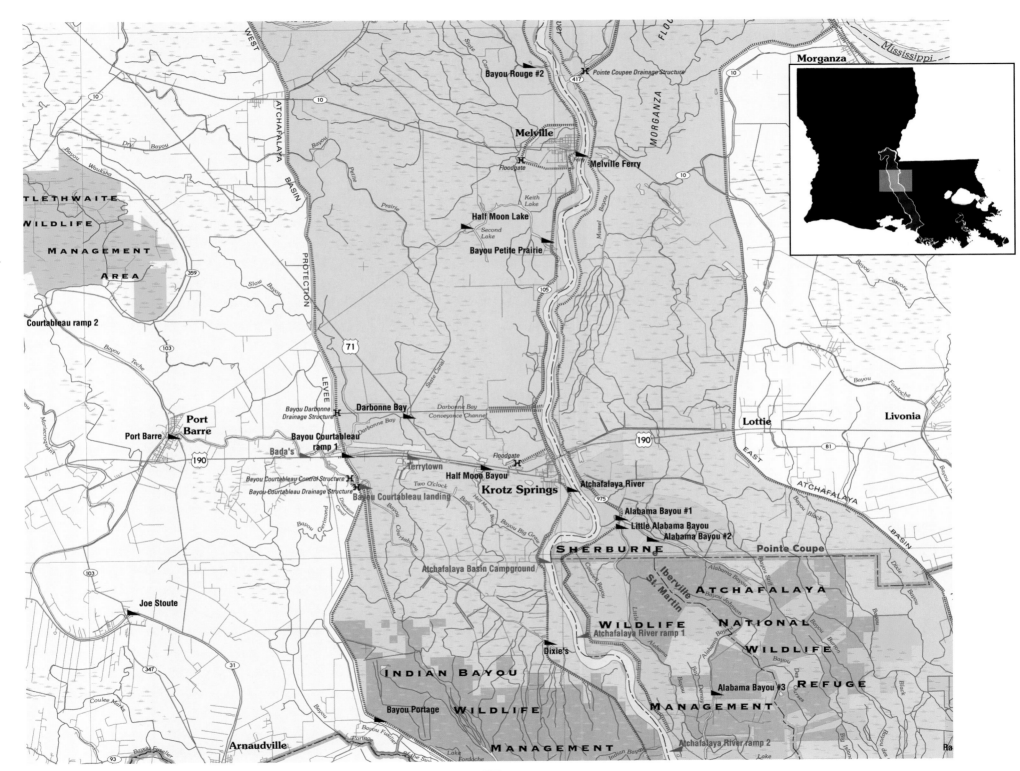

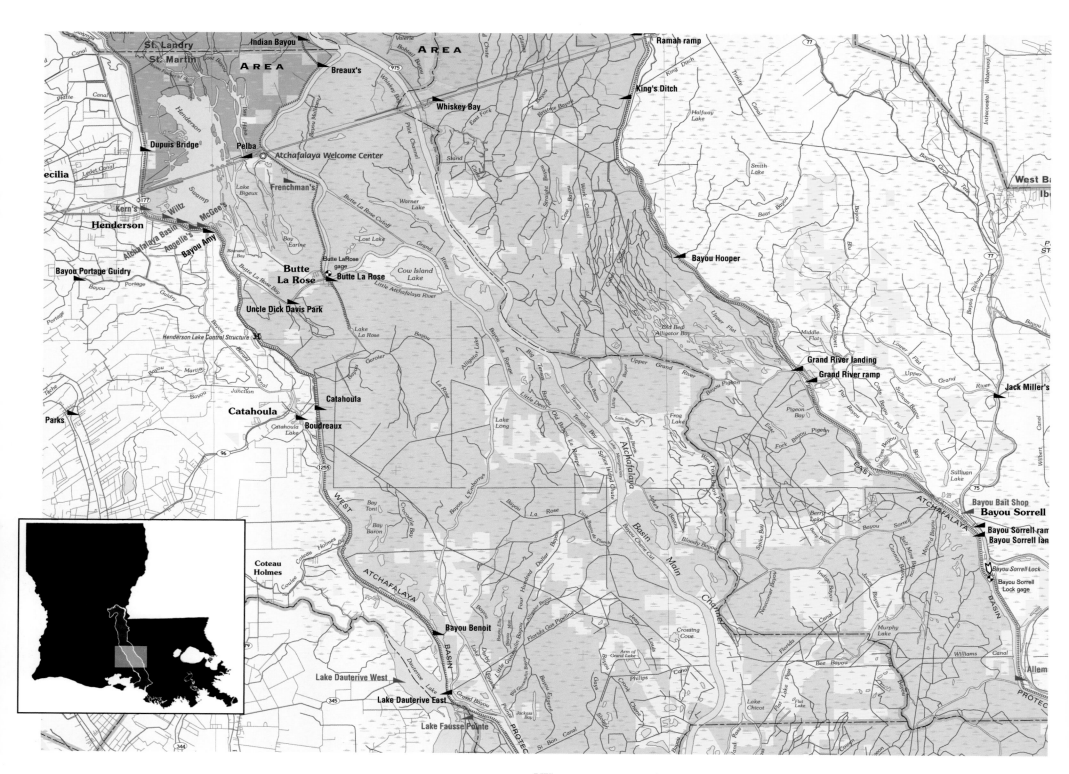

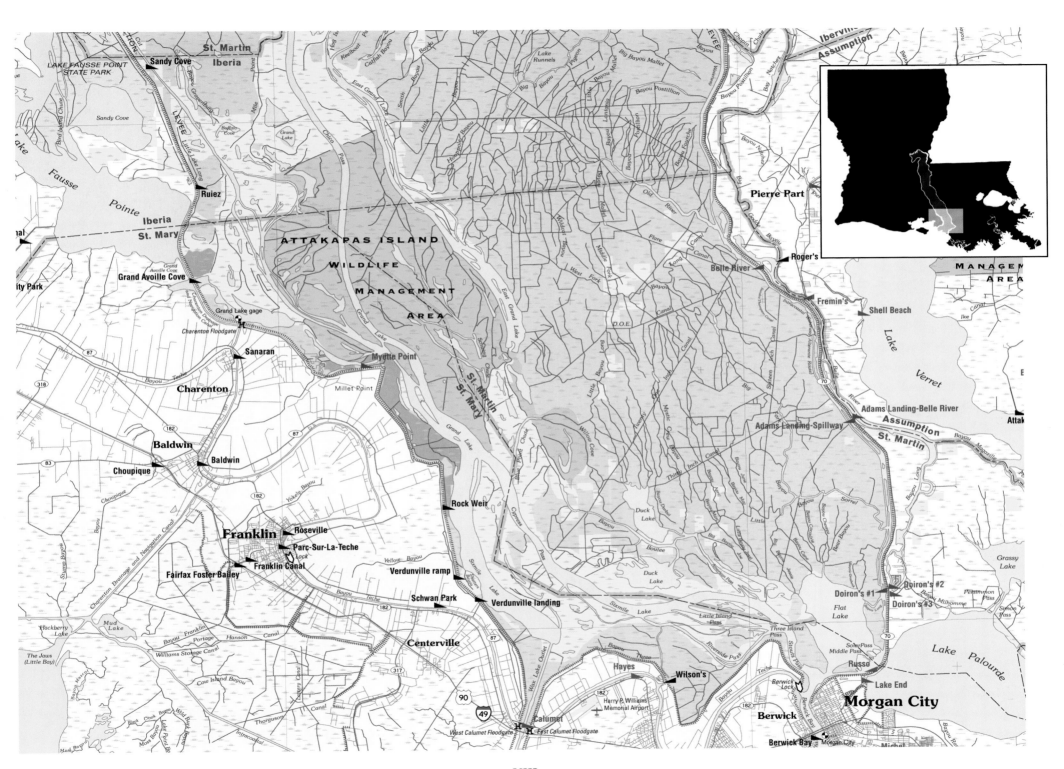

Introduction:
Inheritance and Bayou Chene

On Saturday, September 16, 2006, the 33rd Annual Bayou Chene Reunion took place at Lake End Park, Morgan City. Attendees were commemorating life at a former home place, Bayou Chene, an extinct community that once thrived in the interior of the Atchafalaya Basin.

Since virtually all residents of Bayou Chene left there soon after the closing of its post office in 1952, none but the old-timers at the reunion actually remember living there. But stories are strong, family lineages are still reckoned, memories are shared, heritage hangs on.

The Bayou Chene Reunion was started in 1973, during a year of high water on the Mississippi. That was the year that flood waters nearly caused the control structure at Old River to collapse. There was a lot of talk that year of the entire Mississippi changing course and coming down through the Atchafalaya Basin. Morgan City, and most anything else associated with the Basin, seemed vulnerable. Did the shock of this near catastrophe encourage a wave of nostalgia among the former residents of Bayou Chene?

Thirty-three years before the reunion was established (1940), the Bayou Chene community was alive in the swamp, but it had already begun to dwindle. Annual floods were depositing quantities of silt and sand throughout the lower Basin. Nearly half of nearby Grand Lake had filled with sediment. A huge new levee system completely surrounding the Atchafalaya was nearing completion. The Atchafalaya had transformed into a Spillway.

But, thirty-three years before that (1907), Bayou Chene was in its Golden Age. New internal combustion engines were first placed into fishing boats. The promise of refrigeration and the expansion of transportation led to a boom in commercial fishing. And, at the same time, the timber industry was annually extracting millions of board feet of cypress lumber from the Basin. Work was easy to find; commerce was booming in the swamp.

Stepping back another thirty-three years (1874), commercial fishing was just getting started, and so were large-scale timber operations. In those days, approximately 450 people lived in the Bayou Chene area; most male adults were engaged in logging or related occupations. Back another thirty-three (1841), at least sixteen planters, mostly Anglo-Americans, were homesteading around Bayou Chene. Most were sugar cane farmers who profited from slave labor. Free people of color were finding homes in the area. Back again, to 1808, Bayou Chene was mostly a stop along a water route traversing the Basin from the Mississippi via Bayou Plaquemine to ports and portages along the Bayou Teche. French-speaking Acadians and Spanish-speaking Canary Islanders were looking for homes in the swamp. Before that, and for many generations back, Chitimacha Indians would have been the likely residents of the Bayou Chene area.

Bayou Chene thus serves as a remarkable model for the whole of the Atchafalaya. Traveling back in Bayou Chene history by thirty-three-year increments—about the duration of a healthy human generation

Going many steps beyond general overview, this book also provides a wonderful collection of photographs, interviews, and personal commentaries assembled by Atchafalaya native and renowned author, Greg Guirard. Through Greg's stunning visual artistry and through the narratives he and his Atchafalaya acquaintances share, we are treated to intimate glimpses of the Basin as only an insider could see it. Greg's photos and interviews, all taken during the past several decades, provide us with case studies of interactions between humans and their beloved swamp.

Our overall goal, in the preparation of this book, is to encourage appreciation for the rich heritage of the Atchafalaya. We honor those who are committed to conserving their own traditional lifeways and to sharing their experiences with others. We invite all locals and visitors to learn about and enjoy this natural and cultural treasure. The Atchafalaya is our inheritance; it must not be squandered. Wise approaches to natural conservation must be employed, and many stories must be told.

– C. Ray Brassieur

eration—we encounter an incredible outline of Atchafalaya Swamp heritage. This outline provides glimpses of dynamic environmental changes, technological shifts, and the movements and activities of diverse human populations over time. In many ways, the mere occurrence of a Bayou Chene Reunion in 2006 is quite amazing and special; as mentioned, many attendees at this event had personally never seen the Bayou Chene community. Now, let us project thirty-three years ahead into the future. Will there be a Bayou Chene Reunion in the year 2039? No member of the original community, or even founder of the original reunion, will be living by that time. It will take a lot of good story-telling to conserve Bayou Chene heritage that far into the future, but it can be done.

That is one purpose of this book: to offer a story of the cultural heritage of the Basin, primarily focusing on the activities and lifestyles of everyday folks. Here you will find historic images, brief descriptions of folk occupations, and discussions of landscape and resource utilization. Our intention is to introduce in a general way, to locals and visitors alike, the very rich and complex heritage of a great natural and cultural area.

33rd Annual
Bayou Chene Reunion
Saturday, September 16, 2006
Lake End Park • Morgan City, Louisiana
10:00 a.m. to 4:00 p.m.
Live Music • Jambalaya • T-shirts
Reunion in Memory of Rene' Seneca
(one of the co-founders of this event)

Late nineteenth-century swampers lived in floating camps and traveled the Basin in dugout pirogues. (Unidentified photographer, probably George François Mugnier; courtesy of the Tulane University Special Collections.)

Inheritance from the Past:
Culture History and Folklife of the Atchafalaya

by
C. Ray Brassieur

The Atchafalaya Basin story is a chronicle of dynamic physical and cultural change. To appreciate this great resource we need to consider the environmental transformations that have taken place in this landscape. Environmental change has been accompanied by trends in human settlement patterns and land-use strategies. Certainly, the lifestyles of the people of the swamp are compelling; their daily experiences are unlike those of folks anywhere else in the world. Popular images of the swamp portray it as a Cajun place, and there are many descendants of Acadie in the Basin. But human dimensions of the Atchafalaya are more diverse than that, reflecting a surprising variety of origins, languages, and physical appearances. In this overview we are most concerned with the activities of everyday swamp folk—not that accounts of large-scale industrialists, wealthy speculators, and powerful politicians would be uninteresting—but the occupations, lifestyles, and pastimes of everyday people make the Atchafalaya a very special place for locals and visitors alike. Through the everyday experiences of people over time, a common wetland heritage has been forged in the Atchafalaya. We are the inheritors of that great heritage, and it falls to us to insure that it has a chance to pass down for many generations to come.

Swamp Dynamics: Change is the Only Constant

The Atchafalaya River is the Mississippi's largest distributary stream; its basin holds the largest river swamp in North America. Beginning near Simmesport, the Atchafalaya Basin stretches some 140 miles southward to the Gulf of Mexico. The configuration of this natural basin is the product of a long history of Mississippi delta building. During past millennia, the Mississippi system has transported and deposited enough sediment to build South Louisiana. In so doing, its main channel periodically changes pathways to the Gulf, always seeking a shorter path and a steeper gradient. Once a new course is taken, its mouth advances and pushes steadily southward. But as the river lengthens, its gradient declines; sediment builds up in its meandering

bed. Eventually, the river spills to one side or the other in its quest for a shorter, steeper path to the Gulf.

Floods and their cycles are important in these big river processes. The Mississippi system is a huge funnel draining over 40 percent of the contiguous United States. Winter thaw results in spring floods that swell streams and transport great loads of sediment, eventually flowing through the Mississippi delta to the Gulf. During typical overbank flooding, the heaviest sands and silts are deposited nearest the riverbank. These heavy materials build up to form natural levees, or ridges, offering the best-drained soils in the valley. These natural levees tend to maintain a stable course for the river channel. But periodically, the tremendous power of a flooding river gouges a crevasse in a natural levee, sometimes initiating a course change. Stream piracy also occurs during flood stage: a smaller distributary channel might capture the raging waters of a large river. The Atchafalaya is a pirate; the Mississippi's main channel is her mark.

Currently, the Atchafalaya Basin is bound by natural ridges formed by levee building along active and abandoned courses of the Mississippi River. The western boundary was actively developing between 4,500 and 3,000 years ago, when the Mississippi's main channel flowed along the path now taken by the Bayou Teche. Then, a few hundred years before the birth of Christ, the main channel of the Mississippi was captured from the east, and it flowed in that direction for nearly a thousand years. During the second century A.D., the main channel shifted more directly south to occupy the current channel of Bayou Lafourche. Around A.D. 1000, the main channel sidetracked eastward again, adopting its present course down through and below present-day New Orleans. Within the last century, the Mississippi has been indicating its readiness to move again, this time directly through the Atchafalaya Basin. This new route would cut the river's distance across its deltaic plain by well under half, drowning Morgan City and abandoning the current ports of Baton Rouge and New Orleans. But, for going on two centuries now, behavior of Old Man River and its tributaries has not been determined entirely by natural processes— human agency plays a large role.

"Cypress swamp on the Opelousas railroad." (From *Harper's Weekly*, December 8, 1866.)

"A swamp in Louisiana." (From the *Illustrated London News*, October 23, 1858.)

Major human intervention in the Atchafalaya Basin commenced during the 1830s. In those days, waters of the Red River joined the Mississippi at Turnbull's Bend, several miles above the head of the Atchafalaya River. Serving as a drift chute for the Red and Mississippi rivers, the Atchafalaya's upper section was choked for thirty miles by logs and debris deposited during flood stages. This mass of drift, known as the "raft," rose or fell with changes in water surface elevation. So dense was this mass of debris, so it was said, that herds of cattle could be driven across it. The raft restricted water flow into the Atchafalaya, and it prevented any chance of navigation between the Atchafalaya, the Red, and the Mississippi.

Henry Miller Shreve, U.S. Army Corps of Engineers Superintendent of Western River Improvements, set out to "improve" these conditions. In 1831, he took a modified snag boat and began digging across the narrow neck of Turnbull's Bend. After only two weeks of clearing, the Mississippi took over and gouged a new and shorter channel, which came to be called Shreve's Cut-Off. The abandoned bend, which came to be known as Upper and Lower Old River, began to fill with silt. The Atchafalaya, although still choked at its headwaters by debris, began taking more Red River flow, especially during spring floods. By the end of 1830s, Shreve had completed the removal of 160 miles of snags and obstructions called the Red River Raft, further encouraging Red River flow into the Atchafalaya.

Between 1839 and 1860 a combination of efforts by private citizens and the state of Louisiana resulted in removal of the upper Atchafalaya River raft. As the raft was removed, flow down the Atchafalaya increased. The flood of 1863 apparently broke loose remaining obstructions and the Atchafalaya began to widen and deepen dramatically. During flood seasons, the Atchafalaya began drawing increasingly more water from both the Mississippi and the Red. Throughout the second half of the nineteenth century, Atchafalaya wetland environments—lakes, rivers, bayous, deep-water inundated forests, and flooded backswamps—all greatly expanded. Impacts of Atchafalaya raft removal were incredible and largely unpredicted: navigation between the Atchafalaya, Red, and Mississippi rivers was achieved; a truly awesome wetland environmental regime blossomed;

and, as U.S. Army Major Amos Stoddard had suggested as early as 1812, the likelihood of the Atchafalaya capturing the full flow of the Mississippi River was greatly enhanced.

By the mid-nineteenth century, the Lower Mississippi Valley, and to some extent, the Atchafalaya Basin itself was growing in terms of agricultural, industrial, and commercial development. Frequent, unpredictable, and uncontrollable floods in the Mississippi drainage endangered such development. Levee building, mainly to protect farmlands and plantation assets, had begun during colonial times. The notion grew that swamps and marshes were nothing but "waste land" to be reclaimed and placed in civilized production. But, as the value of developed properties increased, the inadequacy of flood protection became obvious. And, flood protection was expensive. In 1850, the United States Congress passed the Swamp and Overflow Land Act. This plan permitted the federal government to deed millions of acres of swampland to states along the river. States, then, were allowed to sell the acreage to pay for flood control measures. Eight and a half million acres of river swamps and marshes were deeded to Louisiana alone.

Under this plan, flooded timberland in the Atchalafaya Basin, especially thousands of acres of virgin cypress, was sold to large corporations, often for seventy-five cents per acre or less. In return, state revenues from swampland sales resulted in various flood control activities, including construction of a few low levees and periodic operations of state dredge boats—none of these measures significantly reduced flooding in the Atchafalaya. Farmland under cultivation in the Basin, mostly belonging to sugar cane plantations, was subject to increased flooding after 1850. These farms soon failed. On the other hand, flooding was an asset to timber cutters who used high water to float their products to market. Instead of controlling floods in the Atchafalaya, the Swampland Act enabled the complete devastation of one of the world's greatest forests.

Created by Congress in 1879, the Mississippi River Commission, in consultation with the U.S. Army Corps of Engineers, was ordered to prevent destructive floods in the Mississippi Valley. However, the most

destructive flood of the nineteenth century occurred in 1882, breaking the levees in 284 crevasses along the Mississippi. Levee construction began in earnest in that year, but the levee work proved inadequate during the heavy floods of 1912, 1913, 1916, and 1917.

Levees of the 1920s were built higher than their predecessors, but they were proven no more effective by the disaster of 1927—the worst flood of the lower valley on record. The 1927 high water ripped the valley apart. Levees crevassed on both sides of the river from Cairo to the Gulf. Countless bridges, docks, rail trestles, and buildings of every sort were destroyed. Hundreds of people and thousands of animals died—many times that many were displaced. Overbank flooding covered 26,000 square miles, and stayed on the land for as long as three months. The entire Atchafalaya Basin, along with surrounding small-town and rural landscapes, was under water. Displaced Atchafalaya swamp survivors were terrified by this event; personal losses were devastating, and psychological effects long-enduring. Many former swamp dwellers never returned to inhabit the Atchafalaya; within a couple of decades, the swamp emptied of its human residents.

In his superb article, "The Control of Nature: Atchafalaya," published in *The New Yorker* in 1987, John McFee characterizes the Mississippi

Levee crevasse during the 1927 flood.

levee system as an immense empirical experiment that failed, and the flood of 1927 was proof of this failure. As McFee sees it, "the levees were helping to aggravate the problem they were meant to solve. With walls alone, one could only build an absurdly elevated aqueduct." But, in response to the great 1927 flood, more and higher levees would be built. The 1928 Flood Control Act was soon in place. It was an extensive plan for both flood control and navigation on the Mississippi, and it involved an expansive program of levee building.

This 1928 Flood Control Act dramatically expanded the role of the U.S. Army Corps of Engineers. As Martin Reuss claims in his *Designing the Bayous: The Control of Water in the Atchafalalya Basin, 1800-1995,* "the Corps became the primary agent of human change in the Atchafalaya Basin." The scale of that change would be enormous. The Atchafalaya Swamp was transformed into a "spillway" designed to provide a relief outlet for diverted excess Mississippi River water. Enclosure of the Atchafalaya floodway by extensive artificial levees, the straightening of meandering channels, the closing of distributary channels within the Basin, and persistent corrective dredging were important elements in this flood control plan. Between 1932 and 1940, the Atchafalaya channel was enlarged to develop greater capacity, and an entirely new river channel was created between Whiskey Bay and Grand Lake. To provide for maximum discharge of floodwaters

The Old River Control Structure.

potentially beyond the capacity of the Atchafalaya River, a new channel to the Gulf, the Wax Lake Outlet, was dug. Flood control and navigational measures applied to the Basin since it officially became a floodway include dikes, dams, diversion channels, drainage canals, flood gates, pumping stations, navigation locks, revetments, levees, borrow pits, culverts, and hurricane and flood walls. In Reuss's words, "the Corps of Engineers had turned the Atchafalaya Basin into an elaborate plumbing system."

Whether purposefully or not, one result of all this plumbing was to reclaim wetland—to turn swamp into dry land. The newly dredged and straitened channels of the Atchafalaya transported huge volumes of sand during flood stage. Increased discharge of the Atchafalaya River and the Whiskey Bay pilot channel, combined with the restriction of the Atchafalaya flood plain by the artificial levee system, greatly increased sediment carrying capacity. These flood currents released the heaviest of their sediments as they entered the more placid waters of Grand Lake, other lakes of the lower Basin, and smaller meandering bayous. As locals proclaimed, "The sand was coming down from the north." Lacustrine deltas began to form in Grand Lake; virtually the entire lake filled in within several decades. In 1978, Addy Boudreaux from Charenton lamented to me that, as a young man he pulled catfish from Grand Lake hoop nets at the same spot where he later hunted squirrels. Rapid and progressive sedimentation—up to twenty feet thick in some places—quickly increased the total area of bottomland in the Basin at the expense of the wetlands. Lake and deep-water cypress swamp became willow-covered sandy ground. Once started, these processes were unstoppable and irreversible. The swamp's physiography, hydrology, water quality, floral and faunal habitats, and human landscapes changed enormously.

Once the Basin was dedicated as a floodway, the question as to how much flow from the Red and Mississippi rivers should be diverted to the Atchafalaya remained. In 1950, the Atchafalaya was taking 30 percent of the water that came down from the north to Old River. Some of this water originated from Red River drainage, but most of it came from the Mississippi. Pleased that this distribution was desirable, the United States Congress ordered the Corps to preserve and maintain

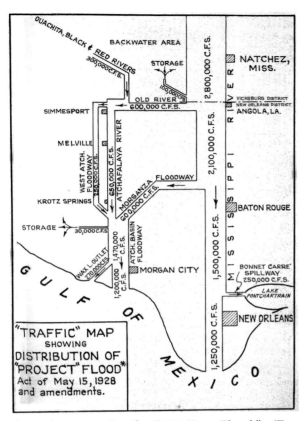

"TRAFFIC" MAP SHOWING DISTRIBUTION OF "PROJECT" FLOOD* Act of May 15, 1928 and amendments.

Hypothetical flood diversion plan for "100 Years Flood." (From *1946 Flood Fighting Plan, New Orleans Engineer District*, U.S. Army Corps of Engineers; New Orleans, 1945.)

these proportions. The Old River Control Structure was authorized in 1954 with a mission to maintain passage into the Atchafalaya of a perpetual 30 percent latitude flow—this was to include all water from the Red River and 25 percent of the Mississippi. The Old River Control Structure went on line in 1963—it met with near catastrophe ten years later. In April 1973, at the height of a huge spring flood, a wingwall on the low sill control structure collapsed and the entire structure was in danger of failure. At the height of the flood, more than a third of the Mississippi was going down the Atchafalaya; had the structure toppled, the flow would have risen to 70 percent and the Atchafalaya would have succeeded in its pirate quest to steal Old Man River.

The Old River Control Structure held in 1973, but high water surges late in that decade renewed fears about its reliability. Authorized in

1979, an auxiliary flood control structure was completed in 1986. This new structure, along with all improvements and repairs, are touted to be fully capable of controlling the mighty floodwaters of the Mississippi. Upon such confidence rides the vitality of Baton Rouge and New Orleans as deep-water ports, the survival of industries and towns in the Atchafalaya Basin, and much more of what we now associate with the cultural and physical landscape of the lower delta. But to some, the flood control structures at Old River signify nothing more than the arrogance of engineers convinced they can conquer the greatest forces of nature. Many believe that the main current of the Mississippi inevitably will take the path of the Atchafalaya—it is simply a question of when, not if.

In addition to the huge impact of drainage and navigational alterations, and significant timber industry activities, the past century has stamped its mark on the Basin landscape in many ways. Oil field exploration, drilling, and production, beginning during the 1930s, established artificial canals and levees, roads, and a variety of production platforms and oil field structures. As the coastal oil industry expanded and eventually moved offshore, beginning in 1947, Morgan City and its surrounding vicinity rapidly industrialized. Today, pipeline rights of way and canals crisscross the Basin from Simmesport to south of Morgan City. Electric transmission lines leave extensive clearings cut through bottomland forest and swamp. Access to and through the swamp has been transformed by huge transportation advancements, like the construction of the Atchafalaya River Bridge on U.S. 190 at Krotz Springs, built between 1931-39; the 17.7-mile "Swampland Expressway," the section of I-10 roadway which crosses the Atchafalaya Basin, completed in 1973; and the recent and ongoing development of US 90 East, the future corridor of I-49.

Born of, and still coupled with, dynamic big river processes, and groomed by years of human interaction, the Atchafalaya is the scene of great physical and cultural change. Yet, it remains an awe-inspiring wetland treasure, and it retains a certain immemorial quintessence felt by those whose experiences and traditions are shaped by it.

The Atchafalaya Basin—a timeless setting. This image the was probably taken between 1900 and 1950.
(Image # 10002; courtesy of the Martin Photo Collection at the Iberia Parish Library in New Iberia.)

People of the Basin

The Original Stewards

Human adaptation to the Atchafalaya began long before the coming of the first Europeans. Archaeological evidence from within the Basin area goes back to the Tchefuncte Period, perhaps 2,500 years ago. It is possible that the earliest of these people inhabited a landscape dominated by the Mississippi when it flowed down the course of the Bayou Teche. During ensuing millennia, floods and alluvial action in the Basin obscured or buried most archaeological remains, though sufficient evidence indicates many centuries of Native American swamp habitation. Indians developed a deep understanding of the swamp and its resources. Their knowledge of landscape features, flora and fauna, and diverse wetland subsistence strategies carried forth into historical times. Such traditional knowledge was shared with colonial immigrants, and some of it persists to this day among Atchafalaya swampers.

As indicated above, most of the Basin's water is now provided by the Atchafalaya River, a distributary for water from the Red and Mississippi river basins. But before man-made diversion of the Red and Mississippi rivers into the Basin, freshwater input consisted almost entirely of local runoff and some overbank flooding from the Mississippi. Generally speaking, the Atchafalaya environment before diversion was much more stable than the present regime. The Basin was occupied for thousands of years by extensive swamps and lakes that were, from the standpoint of natural processes, in a more static or balanced condition. Bayous and rivers within the Basin had relatively stable courses, held in place by oak-covered natural levees. Historical accounts of the swamp abound with descriptions of huge, moss-festooned live oaks; the life span for these oaks covered centuries. The great virgin cypress forest of the Atchafalaya also demonstrates

relative environmental stability; immense time was required for the growth of such a forest—perhaps a thousand years or more.

To be sure, seasonal and cyclical environmental changes in the Basin called for flexibility in the conduct of aboriginal life. Overflow from the Mississippi could be expected from late winter through early summer, causing general water level rise. Interior Basin lands may have been drier from late summer through winter; however, heavy precipitation from either local storms and/or hurricanes could produce flooding in this low country nearly any time of the year. Salinity and water levels in lower sections of the Basin fluctuated with the regular ebb and flow of tidal activities. Water temperature likewise changes with the seasons, even in warm Southern swamps like the Atchafalaya. Fish, crabs, crawfish, and the vast array of coastal fauna adjust their life cycles to such regular environmental changes, prompting the natives to regulate their foraging activities.

A Chitimacha in a dugout pirogue on Bayou Teche, 1908. (Mark R. Harrington, photographer; courtesy of the National Museum of the American Indian, Smithsonian Institution.)

Significant changes in the discharge of channels within the Basin certainly affected prehistoric Indian life. In correlating the relative age of major Indian sites within Iberville Parish, Fred Kniffen, late professor of Geography at Louisiana State University, found that these sites were located in response to changing salinity levels. Kniffen noted the appearance at sites of two different types of shellfish; *Rangia cuneata* (which generally abound in saltier waters) and several species of *Unios* (which grow in fresher waters). Kniffen was able to project the relative development of major distributary channels within and bordering the Basin. As channels such as Bayou Grosse Tete, Grand River, and Bayou Maringouin became major distributaries, they carried greater amounts of fresh water, which caused the *Rangia* to withdraw to areas farther downstream. Indians living on a channel that changed significantly in freshwater discharge eventually had to adapt

their palates to a different type of shellfish, or move to a stream more like their old one.

Indians within the Basin proper located their villages and camps primarily on old natural levee ridges and lakeshores where the best drained soils could be found. Preferred locations for major village sites were on stream confluences and crevasse distributaries that offered access to swamp resources as well as transportation. Deer, bear, various small game, fish, reptiles, waterfowl, plant foods, and shellfish were all extracted from the swamp. Huge cane brakes, consisting of either giant cane (*Arundinaria gigantea*, ssp. *gigantea*) or switch cane (*Arundinaria gigantea*, ssp. *tecta*), sprawled across the Basin, densely growing on the sandier soils of natural levees. These canebrakes provided ideal habitats for game animals and thus prime hunting grounds for the Indians. Important advantages were created by selectively burning canebrakes, Well-drained clearings for camps or villages were made this way, and new tender shoots from a burned over canebrake irresistibly attracted game animals. The river cane itself was essential to aboriginal material culture, providing raw material for woven baskets, mats, wattle-and-mud huts, blowguns, arrow shafts, musical flutes, and many other everyday items.

Chitimachas Delphine Stouff, Clara Dardin (seated), and Octave Stouff, with child, 1908. (Mark R. Harrington, photographer; courtesy of the National Museum of the American Indian, Smithsonian Institution.)

Dr. Mark Rees of the University of Louisiana at Lafayette is currently conducting research on archaeological sites on the western fringe of the Atchafalaya Basin. His interests focus on Indian culture that transpired during the Plaquemine Period, between A.D. 1000 and A.D. 1700. Burial mounds and temple mound complexes were associated with villages during this period. Initial construction of some of these mound complexes began well prior to the Plaquemine Period—C_{14} dates as early as A.D. 700 have been gathered. These villages were located in places that afforded access to wetland resources and to grassy prairie lands flanking the Bayou Teche natural levees. They are also associated with water routes that would have afforded maximum opportunities for water-borne travel and transportation. For centuries, people whose subsistence relied heavily on fish, shellfish, reptiles, birds, deer, and a variety of small mammals occupied these villages. Questions persist as to whether these people grew much corn and/or other plant cultigens. Much remains to be learned about the historical and cultural connections between the residents of these archaeological sites and the known historical Indian tribes of the area.

We know from the earliest historical accounts that Native Americans were associated with the "great swamp." A consideration of Atchafalaya place names confirms this fact. Iberville's first colonial efforts in the Lower Mississippi Valley, beginning in 1699, placed the French in intimate contact with Choctaw and other Muskogean speakers. Choctaw tribesmen served as guides for French explorations of the Mississippi Valley and Gulf Coast. These Indians communicated with other tribal peoples, and with the French, by use of Mobilian, a trade language based heavily on the Choctaw tongue. Thus, many names for geographic features and prominent places throughout Louisiana derive from Choctaw, or Mobilian. Within the Atchafalaya Basin area, some local place names derive from Choctaw terms for Indian tribes that either inhabited or passed through the region—Alabama, Chitimacha, Taensas, Opelousas, Attakapa, and Choctaw are examples. Other Choctaw terms found in the Atchafalaya landscape include: Atchafalaya (*hacha falaia*)—long river; bayou (*bayuk*)—a small river; Catahoula (*oka hullo*)—beloved waters; Chacahoula (*chukka hullo*)—beloved home; Latenache (*latimo hache*)—boggy river; Plaquemine (*piakimin*)—persimmon; and Whiskey Bay (*oski abeha*)—place of the cane.

Some Native American tribes are/were indigenous to the Atchafalaya Basin region—they were there during the time of early historical contact. Other tribal peoples subsequently moved into or through the Basin in response to migratory episodes during the tumultuous history of the Lower Mississippi Valley. Through the generations, Louisiana tribal peoples have endured the consequences of armed conflict, epidemics, forced migrations, social discrimination, and economic marginalization. Tribal amalgamations have occurred, along with many cases of individual inter-tribal and inter-ethnic marriage. It should not be surprising, in this region of mixed and complex heritage, that many locals of Native American descent are unsure of their precise tribal affiliations. Many with Indian blood doubtlessly self-identify as Cajuns, Creoles, or members of some other ethnic community. Still, the Native American story is prominent in the Atchafalaya area, and Indians still reside there.

Chitimacha

The Chitimacha Reservation at Charenton, once better known as Indian Bend, was the first Indian reservation in Louisiana. The Chitimacha have an organized tribal council, a tribal center, a school, and an excellent museum. After gaining federal recognition in 1917, the Chitimacha's reservation lands were placed in federal trust in 1935. Also located on tribal grounds, the highly lucrative Cypress Bayou Casino provides revenue that helps support a wide range of civic and cultural projects. According to the 2000 U.S. Census, a total of 1,001 individuals report Chitimacha identity; another 877 report Chitimacha identity in combination with other tribal or racial affiliations.

For generations, the Chitimacha have been recognized for their superior skills at weaving baskets from split river cane. Beautiful single

Chitimacha Chief Benjamin Paul and children (left to right: Jane Vilcan, Arthur Darden, and Gabriel Darden) with a dugout canoe at Bayou Teche, 1908. (Mark R. Harrington, photographer; courtesy of the National Museum of the American Indian, Smithsonian Institution.)

and double weave baskets, naturally dyed and decorated with traditional motifs, are still being produced today. This tradition is being handed down within certain Chitimacha families; Melissa Darden and her brother John Darden, for example, are carrying forth the artistry of their grandmother, renowned basket maker Lydia Darden. Natural stands of river cane, however, have become rare in the southern Atchafalaya Basin. In response to this shortage, a project has been initiated to establish a sustainable growth of cane on the Chitimacha reservation.

The Chitimacha language has not been spoken in daily conversation for years. The last fluent speaker of Chitimacha, Delphine Ducloux, died in 1940. However, extensive scholarship on the language exists, with major contributions provided by Albert Gatschet, John Swanton, Mary Haas, and Morris Swadesh. During the 1930s, Morris Swadesh visited Charenton and produced wax cylinder recordings of Chitimacha speakers like Benjamin Paul, tribal leader at the time. With assistance from linguist Julian Granberry, linguistic data and early recordings have been used to produce a full dictionary, a smaller word-finder, a reference book on grammar, teachers' guides, and audiocassettes. These materials are being used to teach Chitimacha students in pre-K to eighth grade classes.

The first historical account of Chitimacha Indians dates from 1699 when Iberville agreed to an alliance with them and three other tribes living west of the Mississippi River. During the early eighteenth century, the Chitimacha were recorded as living on Bayou Lafourche and along Grand Lake in the Lower Atchafalaya area. Ethnographer John R. Swanton (1911) argued that three geographically distinct groups spoke the Chitimacha dialect: the Washa, on Bayou Lafourche; the Chawasha, on Bayou Lafourche and on the Mississippi River below New Orleans; and the Chitimacha of the Lower Teche/Grand Lake region. War between the Chitimacha and the French, taking place from 1706 to 1719, commenced following the murder of French missionary, St. Cosme. As a result of this conflict, Chitimacha of the Lafourche region vacated their villages and migrated to join with Chitimacha living in the Charenton area on the Lower Teche.

Historical and ethnographic evidence indicates that the Chitimacha maintained a relatively sedentary lifestyle based on horticulture, fishing, hunting, and gathering of wild resources. They were organized within a fairly rigid social structure composed of endogamous noble and common classes. Hereditary chieftainship typically passed down from father to son. The chief was called *na'ta*, and there is evidence for the historical existence of supra-chiefs who ruled over the chiefs from multiple individual villages. Researcher Christopher Goodwin reported in 1985 that a number of Chitimacha recognize descent from either Fire Chief or Soulier Rouge, both representatives of distinct historic patrilineal lineages. Individuals of high status were accorded special burial rites, and each large village had a charnel house, or *h' na katchi'*, which was tended by a priest called "turkey buzzard man."

In 1815, U.S. Navy timber agent, James Leander Cathcart, observed that Chitimatcha held ceremonial councils at a mound group in Berwick. In 1883, Albert Gatchet listed fifteen villages, thirteen of which were given to him by native informants, two others he assumed to exist based on historical records. James R. Swanton (1911) records six more on the authority of Benjamin Paul, Chitimacha tribal leader in the early 1900s. Swanton's amended list includes the locations of thirteen villages furnished by native sources:

-<u>Teat Kasi'tuneki</u>, now Charenton, on Bayou Teche.

- <u>Ama'tpan na'mu</u>, Bayou Gris, three miles east of Charenton.

- <u>Ne Pinu'ne</u> ("Red Earth"), two miles west of Charenton.

- <u>Co'ktangi ha'ne hetci'ne</u> ("Pond-lily Worship House"), on south side of Graine à Volée inlet, Grand Lake. There was an Indian cemetery and a central house for religious dance here.

- <u>Ne'kun tsi'snis</u> ("Round Island"), a town opposite Lille au Oiseaux, in Lake Fausse Point.

- <u>Hi'pinimte na'mu</u> ("Prairie Landing Village"), on the western part of Grand Lake, at Lake Fausse Point, or on Lake Dauterive.

- Na'mu ka'tsi, Bayou Chene village, St. Martin Parish.

- Ku'cux na'mu, on Lake Mingaluak, near Bayou Chene.

- Ka'me nake teat na'mu, at Bayou du Plomb, near Bayou Chene, eighteen miles north of Charenton.

- Tsa'xtsineup na'mu, on Bayou des Plaquemines, near Grand River, twelve to thirteen miles north of Charenton, the Plaquemine Village.

- Grosse Tete na'mu, (Indian name not remembered), two miles from the Plaquemine village.

- Ce'ti na'mu, west of Plaquemine, on Grand River, the name of which was Ce'ti, twenty miles east of Charenton.

- Tea'ti Kuti'ngi na'mu, at junction of Bayou Teche with Bayou Atchafalaya.

From the distribution of these sites, it is clear that the Chitimacha claimed most of the southern Atchafalaya region as their historical homeland.

Attakapas

During the French Colonial Period, a tribal people calling themselves Ishak occupied settlements dispersed throughout southwestern Louisiana from the Bayou Teche west into east Texas, and from the coast north to the vicinity of Alexandria. These people came to be known as "Attakapas," a Choctaw term that means "man-eaters." As to whether the Attakapas regularly engaged in cannibalism, the historical evidence is extremely thin, and there is no confirmed mention of such behavior in the vicinity of the Atchafalaya Basin.

Archaeologist Jon Gibson suggested that the Attakapas practiced a form of seasonal "transhumance," or migratory foraging pattern. Fragmenting into individual family units during the spring and summer, they lived on shellfish, fish, bird eggs, and aquatic plants. During

The Regis Dardin family, Chitimacha, 1908. (Mark R. Harrington, photographer; courtesy of the National Museum of the American Indian, Smithsonian Institution.)

the fall and winter, they moved inland along major streams, banded together in small semi-sedentary base camps, and hunted and collected acorns. Two eastern bands of this tribe were located along the upper Bayou Teche and in the Vermilion River drainage, and two western bands were situated along the Mermentau and Calcasieu rivers. John Swanton suggested that the Attakapas language was related to Chitimacha and to Tunica-Koroa, though none of these languages were mutually intelligible. It is possible that the Opelousas Indians were a band of the Attakapas, and these two groups may have spoken closely related dialects.

There is no reliable historical evidence of warfare between the Attakapas and colonial settlers, or between these tribal peoples and other Indians. By the mid-eighteenth century, the Attakapas and Opelousa Indians were peaceably engaged in the colonial deerskin trade. During the American Revolution, Attakapas warriors helped Spanish Louisiana governor Gálvez in his campaign against the British. The *American State Papers* document land sales by historic Attakapas chiefs, like Celestine de Tortue, Bernard, and Kinomo, to early French settlers of the Opelousas and Attakapas posts. Some of these lands border the western edge of the Atchafalaya Swamp.

There are no known Attakapas speakers alive today, nor are there any recognized communities of Attakapas. However, an increasing number of individuals claim they are Attakapas descendants, and there are some ongoing efforts to reassert tribal identity.

Opelousa

The Opelousa, who were linguistically kin to the Attakapas, were reported living near Opelousas in 1725, and apparently remained in that area for as long as tribal identity was retained. Some Opelousa may have moved into Spanish Texas after the 1803 American takeover of the Louisiana Territory, others may have been absorbed by the Attakapas, or by one or more Choctaw, or other Native American bands. Wonda Fontenot, in her study of ethnomedicine in the Opelousas area (1994), reports that there were still full-blood Opelousa people in Opelousas in the 1930s, and that some Creoles of Color in St. Landry, Evangeline, and Acadia parishes claim Opelousa ancestry. Although there are no known communities of Opelousa tribal peoples today, historically they inhabited the western fringe of the Atchafalaya Basin, and it is reasonable to assume that descendants still live there.

Houma

At various times during their historical migrations, Houma Indians, and tribal people with whom they amalgamated, have lived near and within the Atchafalaya Basin. Swanton (1946) reports that the Houma were located on the east side of the Mississippi River opposite the mouth of the Red River when they were mentioned in the narratives of La Salle's expedition of 1682, Tonti's of 1686, and Iberville's treaty with them in 1699. Subsequently, the Houma became embroiled in the turmoil that affected so many Native Americans during the colonial days. In 1706, the Tunica, who were at the time living among the Houma, massacred many of them, the Houma taking refuge near New Orleans. Shortly after, the Houma moved up river to Ascension Parish and apparently stayed in that general area until 1776. At some point thereafter, the Houma and remnants of other tribes that they absorbed, moved south to Lafourche and Terrebonne parishes. Members of the following tribes, or others, may have joined the Houma: Acolapissa, Bayougoula, Chawasha, Mugalasha, Quinapissa, Tangipahoa, Washa, Yakne Chitto, Biloxi, and Chitimacha.

The Houma have long struggled for federal tribal recognition. David White, in his *"Cultural Gumbo?": An Ethnographic Overview of Louisiana's Mississippi River Delta* (1998), reports that attempts during the 1990s to register all descendants of historical Houma people succeeded in swelling tribal rolls to around 17,000 members. Houma Indians organized under the United Houma Nation in 1979 and petitioned for federal acknowledgment in 1981. A very slow and eventually unfavorable response was returned to the Houma in 1994, forbidding federal acknowledgment. This response has contributed to factionalism among the Houma people, although the United Houma Nation retains hope for an appeal to the negative finding. Lately, other splinter groups with former ties to the United Houma Nation have formed, seeking federal and/or state recognition. These newer polities include the Biloxi-Chitimacha Confederation of Muskogees and its participants, the Isle de Jean Charles Band, the Bayou Lafourche Band, and the Grand Caillou/Dulac Band. Yet another group, called the Pointe-au-Chien Indian Tribe, has formed out of the same numerous amalgam of tribal peoples, once all called Houma, who inhabit the marshlands and bayous of south Louisiana.

No speakers of original Muskogean languages survive among the Houma; instead, most speak Louisiana French. Many of the Houma who live along Bayou Lafourche and in the Terrebonne Parish marsh make a living from shrimping, continuing to supplement their subsistence by hunting, trapping, fishing, and gathering wild resources. A number of Houma artisans have gained recognition for their baskets, blowguns, carvings, palmetto hats, and other folk items they produce. Recent encroachment of salt water and loss of coastal marsh threaten to displace many Houma communities. Some of these tribal people have moved to the Morgan City area, and many of them shrimp, fish, and hunt in inland and near-shore waters associated with the lower Atchafalaya.

Coushatta and Alabama

Referred to as the Koasati by Swanton (1946), these Muskogean-speaking people of the Creek Confederacy have sustained a complex history of migration from their early homeland along the Tennessee River. Between 1793 and 1795, one segment of the Coushatta, along with some Creek allies of the Alabama tribe, moved into Louisiana and settled on the Red River, and at various locations in southwestern Louisiana. By the time of the Civil War, communities of Coushatta had settled in Allen Parish, along the Calcasieu River near Kinder, and near Elton, a town located some fifteen miles east of Kinder. The Coushatta Indian Tribe of Louisiana obtained federal recognition in June 1973. Today they operate a Coushatta Tribal Center, north of Elton, and a lucrative casino, the Grand Casino Coushatta. There are no known current Coushatta or Alabama communities within the Atchafalaya Basin, although it is likely that the Big and Little Alabama bayous of the Atchafalaya Swamp, north of Butte LaRose, were named after Alabama Indians who passed through the area during their peregrinations.

Tunica-Biloxi and Avoyel

Together with the Chitimacha Tribe, Coushatta Tribe, and Jena Choctaw Band, the Tunica-Biloxi are recognized as a Native American tribe by the federal government. Originally located in the mid-Mississippi Valley, the Tunica moved into ancestral Houma territory along the Mississippi opposite the Red River by 1706 (Swanton 1946). Around 1780, the Tunica, along with descendants of the Biloxi, Avoyel, and Ofo tribes, moved onto the Avoyelles Prairie, where they live today.

The Tunica-Biloxi have a tribal center and museum located near Marksville, in Avoyelles Parish. According to the 2000 U.S. Census, 472 individuals claim Tunica-Biloxi affiliation. Historically and today, these tribal people hunt and fish in the lower Red River and Upper Atchafalaya drainages. Lately, there is interest among some to establish separate recognition for descendants of the Avoyel Indians who live in this area.

Taensas

The Taensas were once a powerful tribe of Nachezean speakers who lived in northeastern Louisiana, on the edge of Lake St. Joseph, in Tensas Parish. They were disturbed from their original homes during the early eighteenth century and began a long and complex migration that traversed south Louisiana several times and included a sojourn near Mobile, Alabama. At some point during the nineteenth century, a group of Taensas Indians moved into the Atchafalaya Swamp and located along bays and bayous at the head of Grand Lake. Big and Little Tensas Bayous are named after this tribal group. It is likely that some of these people intermarried with Chitimacha, Alabama, Attakapa, and/or other non-tribal people, and Taensas blood certainly may run in the veins of Atchafalaya area residents. However, at this time, there is no known movement to claim Taensas identity.

A nineteenth-century landscape scene near the edge of the Atchafalaya Basin, probably on Bayou Teche.

[continued on page 34]

Fountain of Youth (1914)
by Charles Tenney Jackson

In 1914 Outing Publishing Company published a true-life account of two New York businessmen's journey through the swamps of south Louisiana in a native dugout pirogue. The inclusion of over thirty photographs taken during the trip provides an excellent snapshot of what the swamp looked like at that time. Several of the images are published here and on the next page with their original captions.

"Crossing a ridge of the swamp."

"I tried the pirogue out cautiously."

"The trappers paddle from the deep swamp."

"The cypress reflect their beauty from the swamp lake."

"Florion and I hunted squirrels in the deep swamp."

"We dug through the cane to the swamp."

Fountain of Youth (1914)
by Charles Tenney Jackson

"Old Man Captain's camp
after the crevasse."

"The sunken shores and cypress spikes of Grand Lake."

"We climb above the moss plumes
to take an observation."

"Now and then we dragged the
pirogue from pool to pool."

"Running his trapline."

"We shot squirrels along the jungle-
grown shores of Grand Lake

[continued from page 31]

French-Speakers Take to the Swamp

Descendants of French-speaking immigrants from Acadia make up a considerable percentage of the current population living in the Atchafalaya Basin area. But the Acadians (now known as Cajuns) were not the first French speakers in the swamp. Arriving at least twenty-five years before the Acadians, the first Frenchmen came seeking trade with the Indians. Fur trade was important to the early colony, and the Basin forests were rich in furbearers. Whitetail deer were also abundant. As early as 1738, French traders began to capitalize on the deerskin trade. An early post was established on the western fringe of the Basin, east of the current city of Opelousas. Though deer must have been plentiful throughout the Atchafalaya Basin area, the western edge of the swamp offered them special advantages. Going east from the Teche Ridge, and stretching south from Bayou Courtableau to a point near present-day Loreauville, the high grass prairie blended in transition with heavy wetland forests. For deer, this zone of ecological transition was very attractive, offering the cover and mast of the woodlands, along with rich prairie grazing. In 1806, cartographer Barthélémy Lafon identified this long and narrow landscape feature as the "Prairie du Gros Chevreuil" (Big Deer Prairie).

By the early 1760s, ranching was replacing hunting as the primary economic draw to the western fringe of the Atchafalaya. French colonials began to raise cattle in the prairie once renowned for its big deer. *Vacheries* (ranches) were established along the western edge of the Atchafalaya, near the current-day communities of Loreauville and Arnaudville, and in the Opelousas Post area. Pastureland was bought or otherwise acquired from Attakapa or Opelousa tribal leaders. A system of brands was established to mark the cattle that roamed at large on the unfenced prairie. Some local Indians adapted to this new industry either by becoming herd hands for French ranchers or by registering their own brands as independent cattle herders.

It is important to note that African slaves accompanied the earliest French colonists to this region. They shared with their masters the

Man in swamp with large cypress tree and "knees." (Andrew D. Lytle Album and Photograph Collection, Mss. 3708; Louisiana and Lower Mississippi Valley Collection, LSU Libraries, Baton Rouge, La.)

challenges of survival in a distant outpost. Even during the heyday of the deerskin trade, when Opelousas and Attakapas Indian hunters served as the primary procurers of skins, Negro slaves often played important roles as traders. Thus, early French settlement can be viewed in the context of tri-racial partnership. Such partnerships were common along the fringes of the Atchafalaya from earliest contact times. As the economic focus shifted from wild game to cattle, both Indians and Negroes adapted to changing labor needs. For the most part, this system of partnership seemed to work without major conflict. A considerable blending of people and culture has resulted. Today, many French-speaking Creoles living along the fringe of the swamp—people of quite varying skin color —can trace lineages back to these earliest days of frontier settlement.

Acadians came to live in and around the Atchafalaya Basin following several distinct historical periods of migration. The first Acadians to encounter the Atchafalaya region were sent by acting French Governor Charles Phillip Aubry to settle at the Attakapas Post (around St. Martinville), during the spring of 1765. This group of 193 Acadians was led by their chief, Joseph Broussard *dit* Beausoleil. The names of members of this original group are inscribed on plaques in St. Martinville and their descendants are numerous, especially along Bayou Teche and the western edge of the Atchafalaya Basin. Military engineer Louis Andry guided Broussard's group on their westward journey from New Orleans. To traverse the Basin, the Acadians rowed westward from Bayou Plaquemine, followed a tangled series of waterways through the swamp, and arrived at a concession formerly owned by two Frenchmen, Dauterive and Masse, located near present-day St. Martinville. These Acadians were initially established as cattle ranchers. They and their kindred spread out along the Bayou Teche, and eventually throughout the prairies of southwestern Louisiana. From the days of initial immigration to the present, a certain number of Acadians along the western edge of the Basin have maintained a keen interest in the swamp and its resources.

Acadian immigration to Louisiana also had a huge impact on the peopling of the eastern edge of the Atchafalaya. From 1765 to 1769, Acadians settled at various communities along the Mississippi River,

above and below Bayou Plaquemines (an important eastern entrance to the Atchafalaya Swamp). In 1785, nearly 1,600 Acadian immigrants arrived from France. Many of these new Acadian arrivals were settled on unclaimed property along Bayou Lafourche below Donaldsonville. However, during succeeding decades, the competition for prime levee farmland increased along Bayou Lafourche. Many of these newer Acadian arrivals, and/or their offspring, were displaced as small farms were consolidated into larger plantations. Many were forced to move westward to the swampy frontier of settlement in present Assumption and southern Iberville parishes. During the early nineteenth century, the Attakapas Canal was opened from Napoleonville to Lake Verret. This canal provided an alternate route into the swamp and encouraged increased travel and commerce to and from the Attakapas country. Many Acadians who became Atchafalaya swamp dwellers descended from immigrants of 1785 who moved into the Basin from the Bayou Lafourche area.

Perhaps the most interesting Cajun contributions in the Atchafalaya Basin area occurred in the swamp from around 1850 to about 1930. This period—following removal of the Great Raft and continuing until the Atchafalaya Spillway was established in the aftermath of the 1927 Flood—was the "golden era" of swamp life in the Atchafalaya. After 1850, the swamp expanded: river and bayou discharge increased

Family in the swamp, ca. 1895-1900. (George François Mugnier, photographer; courtesy of the Louisiana State Museum.)

greatly during the annual flood, and Atchafalaya lakes and backwaters greatly enlarged. Well established on the fringe of the Basin, and already familiar with its natural resources, Cajuns were poised to take advantage of these dynamic environmental conditions. They became instrumental in the development of the swampland timber industry, and in all of the swamp adaptations that can be thought of as essential to the cultural character of the Atchafalaya.

Today, descendants of French-speaking immigrants from Acadia make up a considerable percentage of the population inhabiting the fringes of the Atchafalaya Basin. Although solid quantitative evidence is scarce, the mere preponderance of known Acadian surnames in the region supports this understanding. As only one of several distinct groups in the Atchafalaya region that share Francophone ancestry, the Cajuns are not uniformly distributed through the region. Distribution of early Acadian settlement patterns suggests that the western and the southeastern fringes of the Basin are more strongly Cajun. Residents with Francophone ancestry in Avoyelles and Pointe Coupée parishes are probably less likely to be descendants of Acadians. Significant early Anglo-American settlement in the Morgan City/Berwick area, and along the levees of the lower Bayou Teche, suggest that Cajun presence in parts of St. Mary Parish may be less apparent. Undoubtedly, the location of the Cajun population within the Basin region has changed over time, and the earliest Cajun settlement patterns may not reliably indicate current distributions. For example, development of Morgan City as an important commercial fishing port, and later as a staging center for the offshore oil industry, attracted the resettlement of many Cajuns to that area. From the mid-nineteenth century until 1927, Cajuns moved into the heart of the swamp to dominate settlement areas like Cow Island, Butte LaRose, Happy Town, Atchafalaya Station, Pelba Station, Graine à Volée Cove,

etc. After the Atchafalaya became a spillway (post-1927 Flood), Cajuns resettled outside of the levee boundaries. Malcolm Comeaux's, *Atchafalaya Swamp Life: Settlement and Folk Occupations* (1972) noted that after 1927 a high concentration of Cajun swamp dwellers moved to the western fringe of the Basin from Henderson south to Catahoula and Charenton. Cajuns from the swamp also resettled in eastern-fringe towns like Belle River, Pierre Part, and Bayou Pigeon.

White Creoles

White Creoles were once a significant and recognizable social group in the Atchafalaya region. Today they are less visible, largely because they have blended into other white populations. During the eighteenth century, the term Creole typically referred to someone of Old World parentage that was born in the New World. Well into the nineteenth century, white Creoles enjoyed elevated social status among Louisiana's Francophone population, and within Lower Mississippi Delta society in general. Although over time the term Creole

A swamp scene, ca. 1895. (George François Mugnier, photographer; courtesy of the Louisiana State Museum.)

took on many new connotations, especially as Louisiana responded to Americanizing influences, a small but socially important group of French-speaking whites continued to self-identify as descendants of the original settlers of the colony.

During the chaotic years of the French Revolution and the Napoleonic era, waves of political refugees from France sought haven in Louisiana. These refugees typically joined into the existing white Creole society. Some moved to the Attakapas Post (St. Martinville), where they established a "Petit Paris" on the Bayou Teche, complete with opera and fashionable entertainments. As described by author George Washington Cable, some sought to maintain their glittering continental life styles. This group cultivated the use of a learned and literate form of French that was carried forth into the twentieth century. During the steamboat era, St. Martinville became a fashionable summer resort for Creoles from New Orleans.

Other white Creoles arrived in Louisiana as refugees from the slave rebellion on the island of Saint-Domingue. Arriving between 1790 and 1810, some of these white Creoles were accompanied by free people of color, and/or black slaves. Both white and black Creoles from the Haitian Revolution settled in the Atchafalaya Basin area, particularly along the Bayou Teche, during the early American period. Anthropologist Jay Edwards of Louisiana State University believes that Haitian refugees are largely responsible for the initial popularity of the shotgun house, the smaller hip-roofed Creole cottage, and many of the larger raised Creole cottages that became popular along the Mississippi River and the Bayou Teche.

Creoles of Color

Black Creoles in southern Louisiana derive from nearly three centuries of contact and synthesis between African slaves, *gens libres de couleur* (free people of color), French and Spanish colonists, Cajuns, and Native Americans, among others. Although, for some, the term "Creole" refers to black Creoles, the terms "Creole of Color" and "White Creole" often are used to avoid ambiguities of reference in a world where race continues to be a significant as a social marker.

In the Atchafalaya Basin region, the largest Creole population resides in the historic Attakapas (St. Mary, Iberia, St. Martin, Vermilion, and Lafayette parishes) and Opelousas (St. Landry Parish) areas. Brasseaux (1996) reports that small numbers of slaves accompanied a few French settlers into these frontier districts during the early 1760s. The appearance of free blacks in this area was reported at the Opelousas Post as early as 1766. During subsequent decades, slaves, many from Francophone West Africa, some by way of the French West Indies, were brought to Bayou Teche to provide labor in the developing sugar industry. Free people of color also migrated into this area, many from the Caribbean during the 1790-1810 period. Slaves in the Attakapas and Opelousas posts were also occasionally freed by their masters to become *gens libres de couleur.* These freed slaves were sometimes the offspring of mixed unions, occasionally sharing blood kinship with former masters. As in all plantation areas of the South, miscegenation was not uncommon, but especially in Louisiana it contributed to the development of a relatively large population of free people of color. Among this population, an elaborate social hierarchy based upon degree of racial mixture developed—higher status being accorded those with less Negro blood. Thus, octaroons (one-eighth Negro), quadroons (one-fourth Negro), and mulattos (one-half Negro), occupied higher social status than pureblood Negroes. Some free people of color became slave owners. Vestiges of this complex social hierarchy persisted into the twentieth century, and may exist in muted form today.

Creole identity along the fringes of the Basin region thus derives from an exceedingly complex ancestral past. Some Creoles recognize Native American ancestry, whether associated with specific tribal affiliation or not. During the colonial and early-American Periods, the Atchafalaya Swamp and its frontier fringes provided settings for communities of Maroons. In addition to runaway slaves, Maroon communities often included displaced tribal peoples and white refugees fleeing the dominant society. Tri-racial ancestry is very common, especially along the western side of the Basin. Today, individual Creoles may choose to emphasize European, African, or Indian ancestry; they may acknowledge a specific mixture of any of these elements; or claim membership in a more-or-less synthetic "Creole" community.

Due to long association with French-speaking people, customs, and lifeways, Creoles are generally quite distinct from other African Americans living in this region—or any other within the United States. English is increasingly the dominant language among Creoles under forty, but French Creole still is commonly spoken along the western edge of the Basin. French Creole, sometimes called "courri-veni," is distinct from other forms of Louisiana French, such as Continental French, or Cajun French, all of which are spoken in this area. Like Cajuns, Creoles tend to be Catholic. However, religion among Creoles may incorporate a blend of Catholicism, African American belief and ritual systems, and Native American medicinal and belief systems. Some elements of Voodoo, representing an Afro-Catholic set of religious practices, remain viable along the western fringe of the Atchafalaya. Strong links between Cajun and Creole foodways, music, dance, and ceremonial practices bespeak a great degree of cultural interaction between these groups. Nick Spitzer (1991) has demonstrated that Creole expressive cultural forms of music, festival, and cuisine mark this cultural group as unique within America but related to other Creole societies in the Caribbean, South America, and West Africa.

Creoles along Bayou Teche and on nearby prairies to the west live in a region which is often referred to as Acadiana, or "Cajun Country." Some Creoles reject the Cajun sociocultural dominance reflected in the naming of the region. The Cajun cultural renaissance, which resulted in the national-level popularity of Cajun music, cuisine, and festivals, has produced a counter-cultural movement among black Creoles. It aims to overturn simplistic popular characterizations of the area as "Cajun." It emphasizes their own distinctive cultural accomplishments, including the highly popular Zydeco music and the distinctive cuisine of the area. Within the past decades official ethnic organizations and events have emerged, such as Creole, Inc. (Lafayette) and the Louisiana Zydeco Festival (Plaisance). A principal aim of the Creole cultural renaissance is to seek equal popular recognition for their many contributions to Louisiana culture, and to compete for the economic benefits of cultural tourism.

English-Speaking African Americans

In many cultural facets, non-Creole African Americans can be quite distinct from their Creole of Color counterparts. These distinctions may include differences in language, religion, food customs, and expressive culture. For example, Protestant churches with rich Gospel music traditions are more common than Zydeco dancehalls in non-Creole African American communities. English-speaking African Americans are largely descended from blacks brought to Louisiana by Anglo settlers in the nineteenth century. As Anglo-Americans purchased plantations in Louisiana, they often brought African slaves and their descendants from other Southern states such as Mississippi, Georgia, Virginia, or the Carolinas. Some of these folks were imported through the slave trade of the Eastern Seaboard, while others came through New Orleans. After 1803, English-speaking African Americans were brought into cotton and sugar growing regions of the state in large numbers. A major influx of immigrants occurred in the late 1820s and the 1830s, when plantations prospered along the Mississippi, Bayou Lafourche, and Bayou Teche. Black populations have tended to remain in those areas where sugar and cotton plantations prospered, although they also migrated to towns such as Lafayette, Opelousas, Morgan City, and Plaquemine.

Prior to 1850, slaves were brought into the swamp to work at sugar plantations established along natural levees within the Atchafalaya Basin. During the 1850s, as water levels progressively rose, plantation economy in the Basin failed and these black farmers left the swamp. After the Civil War, many engaged in sharecropping activities along Bayous Maringouin and Grosse Tete and elsewhere along the fringe of the swamp. For the most part, they did not take up the mixed hunting and fishing economy of the full-time Basin dweller, although many supplemented their subsistence by occasionally hunting, crabbing, and fishing.

"KLEINPETER CAMP" Atchafalaya River.

Kleinpeter Camp on the Atchafalaya River, part of the Louisiana State Penitentiary System, ca. 1900. (Henry L. Fuqua, Jr., Lytle Photographic Collection and Papers, Mss. 1898, Louisiana and Lower Mississippi Valley Collection, LSU Libraries, Baton Rouge, La.)

"FUN IN LEVEE CAMP" Atchafalaya River.

Colonial Spanish and Isleños

A variety of Spanish-speaking colonists immigrated to Louisiana during Spain's rule of the colony (1762-1802), and some of them, and/or their descendants, made their way to the Atchafalaya Basin. Some ninety *Malagueños* (immigrants from Malaga, Spain) settled in New Iberia aduring the years 1778-79. These immigrants initially attempted to cultivate hemp and flax but eventually turned to livestock herding. Other Spanish immigrants came from Granada, Catalonia, and other Spanish homelands in Europe. Still others arrived from Saint-Domingue, or other Spanish-speaking colonies of the Caribbean. The largest and best-documented number of Spanish-speaking immigrants came to Louisiana from the Canary Islands; they became known as the *Isleños*. These Canary Islanders, and their descendants, have had a significant impact in the Atchafalaya area.

Isleños migrated to Louisiana between 1778 and 1783 from their ancestral domain, which consisted of a chain of small islands about sixty-five miles west of the African coast. Spaniards conquered these islands and migrated to them in the fifteenth and sixteenth centuries. During the eighteenth century, Spain recruited young married men and their families from the Canary Islands and sent them to Louisiana hoping to help populate and defend their newly acquired colony. Five of the islands sent recruits to Louisiana: Tenerife (about 45 percent), Gran Canaria (almost 40 percent), Gomera, La Palma, and Lanzarote. The 700 recruits brought their families, increasing the total number of immigrants to 2,373. These immigrants made their passages on six ships that crossed the Atlantic between July 1778 and June 1779. Upon their arrival in New Orleans, Spanish Governor Bernard Gálvez established the Canary Islanders in four different settlements:

- San Bernardo de Galvez, located on shores of the Terre Aux Boeuf in St. Bernard Parish.

- Galveztown, located on shores of Amite River near Manchac in Iberville Parish.

- Valenzuela, located on Bayou Chetimachas (Bayou Lafourche) in Assumption Parish.

- Nueva Iberia (New Iberia), located on shores of Bayou Teche in Iberia Parish .

The settlement at Valenzuela was established, beginning in March 1779, near the present town of Plattenville on Bayou Lafourche below Donaldsonville. For the most part, that stretch of the Lafourche was deserted. But, by 1785, the population along the upper Lafourche began to grow as new Acadian immigrants began to arrive. The Acadian immigrants of 1785 were settled a short distance below the Isleños on Bayou Lafourche. These two Catholic populations mixed readily, inter marrying and sharing cultural traditions. They began to clear and develop small farms on the fertile and well-drained levees of the bayou. With the development of large plantations along Bayou Lafourche during the early nineteenth century, the Isleños, like their Acadian neighbors, were largely displaced. Many established new homes along the eastern fringe of the Atchafalaya Basin along slightly elevated alluvial ridges called brulées, so named because of the burning of native vegetation (usually wild cane) prior to the establishment of new habitations. Other Isleños accompanied their former Acadian neighbors into the interior of the Atchafalaya Swamp, where they found unclaimed land to settle and new ways to subsist.

At the time of migration to Louisiana, Canary Islanders were speaking a native Spanish dialect related to Portuguese. This language has survived among the Isleños of St. Bernard Parish. Spanish language and customs were maintained for some time along the eastern periphery of the Atchafalaya, but the Isleños there eventually assimilated, for the most part, into the French-speaking Cajun group. Today, most descendents of Spanish colonial immigrants in the Basin area are likely to consider themselves Cajuns.

"The floods in the Teche Country, Louisiana." (From *Harper's Weekly*, March 29, 1884).

Les Américains: Anglo-Americans, and other English-Speakers

Generally speaking, entry of English speakers into south central and southwestern Louisiana proceeded at a relatively slow pace until well after the Louisiana Purchase; however, pioneer Anglo-American settlement in the lower Atchafalaya began during the late eighteenth century. In 1797, Thomas Berwick from Pennsylvania, a surveyor who had worked extensively for the Spanish government, settled on the west bank of the Atchafalaya near present day Morgan City. Around 1809, Walter Brashear, a physician from Kentucky, moved across the river from Berwick and became a large planter. By the early 1800s, slave labor was being employed in this area for the production of cotton and sugar. These and other Anglo-American settlements were oriented to agricultural lands along the natural levees of streams that converge in this area, including the Atchafalaya River, Bayou Boeuf, Bayou L'Ours, Bayou Black, Bayou Shaffer, and the lower Bayou Teche. Prior to the Civil War, large-scale farming was expanding to the better-drained natural levee soils of the interior of the Basin. Plantation agriculture and commerce prospered from the Atchafalaya's ample network of inland water transportation routes, which included shipping access to the Gulf of Mexico.

Many of the English-speaking settlers of the Lower Atchafalaya were of Scotch-Irish or English descent, although some derived from English, Irish, Welsh, German, or Dutch stock. They can be called "Anglo-Americans" in the sense that they generally were not direct immigrants to South Louisiana from a European mother country. Instead, most came from Upland South states like Mississippi, Alabama, Georgia, Arkansas and Texas. Others came from the Tidewater and Piedmont areas of Maryland, Virginia, and the Carolinas, some by way of Tennessee and Kentucky. Still others arrived from Pennsylvania and the New England states.

Descendants of earlier colonial stock, predominantly French speakers, typically referred to any and all of these Anglo-Americans as *les Américains*. But, they were quite diverse as an ethnic group. Social class, in particular, was noticeable as a point of differentiation among English speakers. On one extreme were the large planters, oriented towards large-scale cash cropping, mass agricultural labor, mechanized transportation, and market development. Occupying the upper levels of the socioeconomic hierarchy, they tended toward leadership in local and state politics, civil and legal authority, social and educational institutions. These were the builders of grand Greek Revival plantation houses, with central hallways and monumental gable-front porticos, many of which can still be seen in St. Mary Parish.

At the other end of the spectrum was a variety of Anglo-American yeoman farmers, pioneers searching for homesteads, and squatters. Many of these immigrants were Scotch-Irish Presbyterians from the Upland South. They typically represented a highly independent and self-reliant form of culture, with little trust or interest in civil authority outside of their own neighborhood. Many preferred to live in small, isolated, dispersed settlements. Some of these folks were highly adaptable to new environments, and they found the interior of the Atchafalaya to their liking. They thrived on a flexible subsistence pattern based on small-scale, free-range hog and cattle husbandry, gardening, and swamp resource gathering. By the mid-nineteenth century, the removal of the Atchafalaya raft and the opening of the Mississippi and Atchafalaya River confluence was providing another vector of Anglo-American immigration into the swamp. These Anglo fishermen and their families were already well adapted to wetland and water-related lifestyles of the Mississippi. Descending into the Basin to take advantage of its expanding fisheries, these self-reliant English-speakers melded well, for the most part, with the Cajuns, Native Americans, and other Anglos already living there.

Bayou Chene, the largest community in the interior of the Basin, became a predominantly Anglo enclave after the Civil War. Although it remained ethnically diverse, English speakers eventually dominated the lower Atchafalaya. Cultural conflicts between Protestant Anglos and Catholic Cajuns were not unknown. However, generally speak-

Moss picker's cabin, ca. 1895. (George François Mugnier, photographer; courtesy of the Louisiana State Museum.)

ing, residents cherished the advantages of swamp life enough to set aside historical prejudices and linguistic differences. After the flood of 1927, many of the former residents of the Bayou Chene area moved to Bayou Sorrel, where Protestant, Anglo culture has maintained its distinctive features. As the twentieth century progressed, a number of factors coalesced to insure that the English language would dominate throughout the Atchafalaya Basin area. The most potent of these factors included the establishment of English-only mandatory education; the development of the petrochemical industry and its associated influences; and the decline and dispersal of traditional French-speaking swamp communities.

Italians

Though Italian immigration into the Atchafalaya area was a relatively late phenomenon, it was important to the eventual cultural makeup of the area. By 1880, the sugar industry of Louisiana was in need of new sources of labor. By coincidence, an economic depression in Italy

prompted large groups of landless farmers to seek a better living in the New World. Italian immigration to Louisiana peaked between 1880 and 1910. During this period, Louisiana labor brokers in New Orleans recruited workers largely from Sicily and southern Italy. By 1910, higher wages available in Italy altered this immigration pattern.

Some immigrants went directly to work as craftsmen or laborers, though many eventually found occupations as truck farmers and small merchants. In the Atchafalaya region, some Italians found a niche in the distribution of groceries and merchandise by horse-drawn cart. Merchant routes were strategically developed to respond to the needs of pre-mechanized, small-scale, rural farming and fishing communities. The age of motorization and refrigeration brought new opportunities to Italian merchants as they established stores to serve the growing towns and villages surrounding the Atchafalaya Basin. Those merchants who developed the capacity to supply ice to the local commercial fisheries did particularly well. Thriving Italian-owned businesses developed in Morgan City, Morganza, Maringouin, St. Martinville, and other towns on the fringe of the swamp.

Mechanization was not as advantageous to many Italian truck farmers. Following the Second World War the increase in machine technology led to increased farm size and decreased need for farm labor. Small farmers, including many Italians, were generally unable to compete with larger plantation owners in the race to mechanize. Many moved off the land and into nearby towns and cities. Descendants of this group are to be found in all of the parishes touching upon the Atchafalaya Basin.

Today, they continue to operate small businesses, groceries, and restaurants, though many hold professional positions in fields of medicine, law, or public service. Italian descendants frequently have intermarried with members of other ethnic groups. To a large degree, they have made accommodations to dominant local cultural patterns. Acculturation to Cajun culture in the Atchafalaya area was furthered by their shared Catholic religious affiliation. Italian cuisine, which is popular throughout southern Louisiana, has been significantly "creolized" in the Atchafalaya region—look for plenty of cayenne in the red sauce.

The Saint Joseph's Day feast tradition is an important Italian cultural contribution to southern Louisiana. Originally a Sicilian tradition based largely in New Orleans, it spread widely throughout French Louisiana in the years following World War II. Saint Joseph altars are "pledged" and erected in private homes and public places in order to share good fortune with those in need. Great amounts of energy are applied to preparation of elaborate and decorative bakery items and food dishes that are displayed on these altars. Catholic religious symbolism is central to this custom, but it also can be seen as a vibrant expression of contemporary regional Italian heritage. These altars are displayed annually in all major towns in the Basin vicinity.

Asians

The Atchafalaya Basin area is home to a variety of peoples whose ancestry derives from regions of Asia. These people certainly are not all members of one distinct ethnic group; rather they represent many distinct national origins, language communities, and migratory histories. Some of the earliest Asian immigrants to Louisiana were Filipinos. By the 1820s, some Filipinos were settled in stilt villages such as St. Malo, located on the edge of Lake Borgne, south of New Orleans. Later during the nineteenth century, they specialized in shrimp drying platforms elevated above water on wooden piers. Manilla Village, located in western Barataria Bay, was the most famous of these platform settlements. Relying heavily upon coastal resources and boats, Louisiana Filipinos made important contributions to the technologies and lifeways of coastal Louisiana. Subsequent waves of Filipino immigration to Louisiana followed both the Philippine-American War (1899-1902), and World War II. Traditionally Catholic, Filipinos tend to participate fully in the culture of French Louisiana. Although most Louisiana Filipinos live in the New Orleans area, or in coastal regions south of the city, smaller groups are found in Houma and Morgan City.

A variety of Chinese and Japanese peoples have also migrated to south Louisiana. The earliest Chinese arrived largely from the West Indies during the 1860s. These Chinese had been previously employed by the Spanish as sugar cane farm laborers, mainly in Cuba. They were needed in Louisiana as a result of a labor shortage prior to the American Civil War. Numbers of Chinese farm laborers from the Caribbean and elsewhere were brought to the Bayou Lafourche area. However, few Chinese remained as field laborers after their initial contracts were fulfilled. During the last decades of the nineteenth century, Chinese immigrants entered Louisiana from Hong Kong, the Philippines, California, and elsewhere. Relatively small numbers of Japanese immigrants were coming to Louisiana at the same time. Some Chinese and Japanese turned to small businesses in the New Orleans area; others turned to fishing and shrimp drying, establishing shrimp drying platforms in Barataria Bay. Both the Chinese and Japanese deserve credit for popularizing the use of dried shrimp, which remains an important item in Louisiana coastal cuisine. In general, both the Chinese and the Japanese of the Atchafalaya Basin area live in small family groups that are occupied in restaurant or other small businesses.

Perhaps the most successful Asian immigrant group in the Atchafalaya Basin area is Vietnamese. Most of them arrived in Louisiana after the fall of South Vietnam to Communist forces in 1975. Many of these immigrants came from fishing families, and they have specialized in Louisiana's seafood industries. During the past thirty years, the Vietnamese have come to dominate the Louisiana coastal shrimping and crabbing industries, with their large, modern, steel-hulled shrimp boats. In the Atchafalaya area, Vietnamese have largely displaced Cajun workers in the crawfish and crab processing industries. Large Vietnamese communities are prominent along the western edge of the swamp, especially in the vicinity of Henderson. Other large communities live on the lower Bayou Teche, in the Morgan City area, and in Ascension Parish. They are increasingly successful as seafood wholesale and retail merchants, and they also excel in the marketing of garden produce, and in a wide variety of small businesses. Louisiana-born Vietnamese students, especially of the first generation, fare exceedingly well in education, and they apply their college training in a variety of professional occupations.

Other Southeast Asian communities have also made homes in the Atchafalaya Basin area. A large Laotian community developed in Iberia Parish in the early 1980s. After the Vietnamese, the Laotians are the second largest Southeast Asian group in Louisiana. A New Year celebration is a highlight of the Laotian calendar. It takes place on Easter weekend and features food, dance, music, and costume. Immigrants from Cambodia, Thailand, and elsewhere in Southeast Asia also live in the Atchafalaya area. In all of their diversity, Asian immigrants and their descendants are coming to represent what some call "Louisiana's Asian Gulf Coast."

Tapping Swamp Resources

Foraging for natural resources has been an ancient pursuit in the Atchafalaya, one carried forth by some swampers to this day. Indians and later generations of swamp dwellers took full advantage of the swamp for small-scale household subsistence needs. But, since the early days of the colony, commercial interests also began to focus on swamp resources. As mentioned, French commercial interests first organized around the deerskin trade. Cattle ranching was established during the second half of the eighteenth century, and it has continued as a moderately important commercial concern into the present. Cattle herding in the swamp must constantly respond to dynamic wetland conditions. For the swamp herder, sometimes boats are more important than horses, and rubber waders more useful than cowboy boots.

Farming

The *brulées*, old natural levees that bordered the swamp, were occupied by Acadian (and Spanish) agriculturalists sometime after 1770. The Acadian farmers were largely subsistence farmers who grew only a little cotton to be sold commercially. The first recorded large-scale

Man standing in cypress tree, ca. 1900. (Andrew D. Lytle Album and Photographic Collection, Mss. 3708, Louisiana and Lower Mississippi Valley Collection, LSU Libraries, Baton Rouge, La.)

commercial plantations in the Atchafalaya Basin were on agricultural lands near the current site of Morgan City, and along the natural levees of the lower Atchafalaya and Bayou Boeuf. By 1819, slave labor was being utilized in this area for the production of cotton and sugar.

Rapid development of farming around present-day Morgan City resulted not only from the availability of ample and rich natural levee soil but also because the area was located on water routes through the Atchafalaya Basin. Once steam power had been adapted to transportation and farm mechanization, a strong agricultural presence spread along Bayou Teche and in St. Mary Parish.

Within the interior of the Basin, farming developed slowly. By the 1830s, the plantation system began to expand into the interior. One of the first areas to develop during this period was the fertile levee lands along bayous Grosse Tete and Maringouin. Black labor is still used in this area to maintain large cane and soybean farms. Plantation agriculture soon spread to other areas of the Basin. Large cane operations were established along Bayou Chene, Bayou Sorrel, Bayou Pigeon, Grand River, and around Pierre Part and Belle River. Slave owners who bought land south of the present U.S. Highway 190 typically grew cotton as a cash crop. Cotton plantations were scattered on the Alabama and Little Alabama bayous, and Bayous Johnson and Des Ours. These plantations of the Atchafalaya interior generally produced poorer crops than those grown on the natural levee soil surrounding the Basin, and they were constantly threatened by inundation.

Not long after the Civil War, however, agriculture began to decline rapidly in the Basin. Damage inflicted on plantations by Union soldiers and the freeing of the slaves must be considered as major causes for this decline. However, agriculture within the interior of the Basin was also negatively affected by the occurrence of floods resulting from the clearance of rafts in the upper portions of the Atchafalaya. This increased flooding forced the abandonment of agricultural areas in the heart of the Basin and made farming enterprises on the fringe of the Basin extremely risky.

Ironically, as a long-range effect of this increased flooding, progressive sedimentation from overbank deposits eventually built bottomlands suitable for farming. Especially in upper and middle sections of the Basin, large-scale farming operations were established in previously flooded locations. As siltation progresses, agricultural interests have focused increasingly on the middle, and to some extent, on the lower Basin. Unfortunately, modern farming techniques are presently endangering other swamp resources. Water quality has been affected by farm erosion. Aerial spraying of pesticides and herbicides, as well as chemical runoff, poses serious dangers to swamp flora and fauna.

Adaptations to a Growing Swamp

Adaptation to the swamp during the late nineteenth and early twentieth centuries was characterized by an amazing diversity of economic activities. In his *Atchafalaya Swamp Life* (1972), Malcolm Comeaux describes and illustrates the annual round of folk activities in the Basin. The goal of many of these activities was personal and family subsistence—producing food for the household table. Some jobs earned money, but many swampers lived on the bare margins of a cash market economy. Swampers gathered Spanish moss and caught catfish and crawfish during the spring; seined, frogged, crabbed, and caught turtles during the summer; continued fishing, caught alligators and began hunting in the fall; and continued hunting and fishing as they took up trapping in the winter. Honey, blackberries, muscadines, persimmons, and many other wild edibles were gathered in season. Floating camp boats, which were usually owner-built, allowed swampers to relocate as necessary to take advantage of seasonal opportunities. Tremendous knowledge of natural resources and close integration with the Basin environment permitted a diversity of economic strategies and an independent lifestyle among swamp dwellers. Human qualities of flexibility and resourcefulness became primary tools for success. Passed from one generation to the next, these qualities still characterize the descendants of the swampers.

Wetland Lumber Industry

The first lumber operations in the Basin began well before the Civil War and relied upon folk techniques. However, as the flooding regimes expanded during the second half of the nineteenth century, lumbermen readily adapted to the seasonal vacillation of conditions in the swamp. In the fall, trees were "ringed" with an axe in order to remove the sap. During the spring flood these deadened trees were

[continued on page 51]

South Louisiana Logging Scrapbook

All of the images on this and the next page were taken by Baton Rouge photographer Andrew D. Lytle, circa 1890-1905. (Andrew D. Lytle Collection, Mss. 893, 1254, Louisiana and Lower Mississippi Valley Collection, LSU Libraries, Baton Rouge, La.)

This image and all of those on the next two pages were taken by New Orleans photographer George François Mugnier, circa 1895. (Courtesy of the Louisiana State Museum.)

South Louisiana Logging Scrapbook

[continued from page 45]

cut and floated to the sawmill. This technique was specifically developed for the gathering of "natural floaters" like the cypress and tupelo gum that grew in virgin profusion throughout the Basin.

As the wetland environment increased, subsequent to the removal of the raft, this technique began to be profitable on a large scale. By 1870, large crews of lumbermen—some local inhabitants, some Northern lumberjacks, and many blacks from the surrounding agricultural lands—began to harvest the great forest. The cut timbers were fashioned into rafts and floated to lumber mills that sprang up throughout the Basin. Large mills existed in places like Patterson, Morgan City, and Franklin, around the present city of Plaquemine, and at Sherburne, an extinct community near Krotz Springs.

Technological advances in the last half of the nineteenth and early twentieth century boosted the lumbering industry into a highly efficient, if somewhat devastating, operation. The overhead skidder and the pull boat allowed millions of board feet of lumber to be rapidly extracted from the Basin. Rapid transportation of felled timbers was provided first by steamboats and later by gasoline-powered boats. An extensive system of rails and trams was built in many places to speed the process. For the individual timber cutter, the move from *passe-partout* (two man cross-cut saw) to power-driven chain saw was a huge advancement that occurred during the 1930s. By 1927 the great red cypress forests were depleted. Although other species such as oak, cottonwood, wil-

Floating logs down Bayou Teche to the sawmill. (Image # 10001, Courtesy of the Martin Photo Collection at the Iberia Parish Library in New Iberia.)

low, and gum continued to be logged on a smaller scale, the days of the great Atchafalaya lumber industry were over.

Increased sedimentation in the Basin seriously damaged some timber resources during the last half of the twentieth century, killing entire stands of trees. The ongoing increase in bottomland areas at the expense of the wetlands also led to changes in logging technique. The old method of floating the logs out during the spring flood was replaced with a network of roads built through the forest and trucks to haul the cut timber. In many areas, large-scale agricultural operations replaced the forests. In areas covered with thick layers of sand, like the filled-in bed of Grand Lake for example, new growths of black willow have sprung up. These extensive willow forests are markers of the huge environmental changes that followed the passing of the great cypress swamp. No large-scale economic use has been found for these willows.

Some cypress remains in the Atchafalaya today, typically found in flooded backwater environments. These trees represent the new growth that followed the cypress harvest. Some of them may be approaching eighty to one hundred years old—they could have been upstarts when their centuries-old parents were removed during the early twentieth century. These young trees are called gros-bec cypress. Their wood is not prized as lumber; it is not everlasting like that of ancient first-growth cypress. Yet, these younger trees represent the seedlings of the great cypress forest of the future. For that reason they are cherished by those who know of the grandeur of such things. But, some timber cutters are moved by neither nostalgia nor the promise of future forests. In some places, young cypress trees are now being cut and made into mulch for decorative landscaping material, a practice that fuels controversy between private landowners and conservationists.

Trailing Sinkers

After the great cypress boom was over, an interesting "cleaning up" industry developed. As mentioned earlier, the method used to extract logs from the swamp environment relied heavily upon seasonal changes in water level. The purpose of ringing the trees with an axe in the fall was to allow the sap to drain out. When the spring floods arrived the deadened trees could be cut down and floated to the mills. Quite often, however, a lumberman would fell a tree during the spring flood only to find that not enough sap had escaped from the tree to permit buoyancy. These trees would sink into the floodwaters and be impossible to move to the mill. Whenever the loggers realized that they had cut a "sinker," they would attempt to connect it to a raft made

of good "floaters." Occasionally, much to the disappointment of the loggers, the sinker would drag down the entire raft.

As siltation increased in the Basin, these sinkers were covered with sediment, making their retrieval too costly for the lumber companies to pursue. Crafty residents living on the fringe of the Basin soon developed methods to retrieve these sinkers. A group of men would "trail" through the swamp during low water looking for likely rises in the terrain. A hole was then dug to verify the location of the sinkers. Next, a trench was placed across the rise wide enough to permit the seven-foot *passe-partout* (two-man cross-cut saw) to be lowered onto the logs. Once the log was cut, a team of mules would be hitched to the log that was then pulled to the sawmill.

A variation of this technique developed using the spring floods to facilitate removal of the sinkers. After the sinkers had been freed from the earth, they were rafted together and tied to a set of pontoons made of good floaters. When the yearly flood came, they were then pulled to the mill by a small motorboat. As one could imagine, trailing sinkers was a tremendously hard job. It was accomplished most often by poor swampers who could not afford the price of lumber. To have these sinkers cut into usable planks, swampers often had to give half of the milled lumber to the sawmill. Yet, despite difficulties, many wood-frame cypress houses on the edge of the Basin today were built entirely of cypress heartwood extracted from the swamp in this manner.

Cypress sinker wood is still an essential commodity to a small, but resilient group of traditional wooden boat builders. Virgin cypress, no matter if it has been felled and sunk for over a century, is still considered the best stock for wooden boats. Swampers still trail sinkers in search of these treasured remains of an ancient industry. Choice logs are typically milled on small-scale, privately owned band saw mills that can produce planks up to three-feet wide, or so. Virgin cypress lumber is becoming increasingly rare and expensive, but the demand remains high.

In addition to the sinker salvage operation, specialty wood resources are sought for a wide variety of purposes. Driftwood, pieces of old timber, odd knotty trunk sections, and cypress roots are sought by artists and artisans who produce picture frames, sculptures, and various expressions of art. Sections of swamp tupelo gum (*Nyssa sylvatica var. biflora*) are harvested to supply stock for the carvers of waterfowl decoys. Decoy carving is a highly developed art form in south Louisiana.

Fin Fishing

Fishing in the Atchafalaya Basin is an extremely old industry, having been important as a means of subsistence to the Indians of the region. As Europeans began to move into the swamp during the early 1800s, fishing for local consumption continued to be significant. Removal of the raft and subsequent increasing severity of floods throughout the mid-1800s significantly contributed to the lifestyle of fishing swampers.

By 1873 commercial fishing had begun in the Basin. The development of the tow-car, a large flat-bottomed skiff that permitted free circulation of water through the hull, allowed live fish to be transported out of the Basin. Late nineteenth-century improvements in the railway system, including the development of refrigerated rail cars, as well as the availability of manufactured ice, led to rapid development of the commercial fishing industry. By the turn of the twentieth century, commercial fishing was a booming enterprise in the Atchafalaya Basin. Morgan City, Plaquemine, Melville, and eventually Atchafalaya Station (after the Southern Pacific Railroad line between Baton Rouge and Lafayette was completed in 1906) all became important terminals for Atchafalaya fish commerce. Fish-buying boats would make long routes to campboat villages in the swamp, purchasing or trading for the local catch. As commerce developed, Atchafalaya fish was eventually distributed by rail throughout the country.

A variety of fish are caught in the Basin for commercial use. The catfish became the most avidly sought by most commercial fishermen. This delectable catch is sold as a specialty in restaurants through-
out the South. The eel catfish (*Ictalurus punctatus*), also commonly known as the channel cat, became a major commercial catch. French speakers call it *barbue* or *barbotte*. Blue catfish (*Ictalurus furcatus*), were likewise poplar in commercial trade. However, the Opelousas catfish (*Pylodictis olivaris*), sometimes known as flathead, yellow, or spotted catfish, is the king for many Atchafalaya fishermen. Local French speakers call this fish the *goujon* or *machoir-ronde*. Commercial fish buyers prize the Opelousas, but it is often retained by the fisherman for table fare—too good to sell. At any rate, the market for wild Atchafalaya catfish has suffered significantly because of the rise of aquaculture. Standard-sized, pond-raised catfish fillets fill the seafood cases at major grocery stores.

The buffalofish (particularly *Ictiobus cyprinellus*) also became important to the commercial fish industry of the Basin. Unlike the catfish, almost all of the buffalofish catch was exported outside of the state. Rarely, if ever, are buffalofish advertised as a specialty at local restaurants. However, this fish was, and still is, used for household consumption by some locals who know how to cook and eat bony fish—it makes a very tasty stew. Because of the decline in both local and export markets for buffalofish during the past decades, this fish is used more often today as cut bait for local crawfishing, crabbing, and line fishing.

Another fish once commercially important is the gaspergou, or fresh water drum (*Aplodinotus grunniens*)—*casse burgot*, in French. There is a local market for the gaspergou, though it has declined in recent years. Twenty years ago, gaspergou *courtbouillon* (fish stew) was offered on the menu at seafood restaurants in Atchafalaya communities like Henderson; it is no longer easy to find. It is still found as the main attraction at local church fairs and fish suppers among friends.

Besides the gaspergou, another Atchafalaya fish that enjoys a loyal, if relatively small, local market is the gar. There are several species of these caught in the Atchafalaya: the alligator gar (*Lepisosteus spatula*), the longnose gar (*Lepisosteus osseus*), the shortnose gar (*Lepisosteus platostomus*), and the spotted gar (*Lepisosteus oculatus*). The alligator gar in one of the largest freshwater fishes in North

America. It commonly grows to a size of 6.5 ft. and over 100 lbs., but it has been reported to grow up to 350 lbs. and around 10 ft. in length. Gar are often caught on jug lines, sometimes netted, caught on rod and reel, or shot by bow hunters. Local fish markets sell gar seasonally, though larger commercial grocery stores rarely carry it. Local residents of the Atchafalaya area are fond of gar cooked in *court-bouillon*, barbequed, baked, or rolled into garfish balls (*boulettes de poisson armé*).

The choupique, also called grinnel, or bowfin (*Amia calva*), is another fish rarely seen in grocery outlets, but nevertheless enthusiastically caught and eaten by some locals. Within the past five years, a minor industry has developed around the production of choupique eggs into a "caviar" substitute. The flesh of the fish is typically wasted during this harvest. The potential negative effects of this industry on the choupique population, and the potential for larger ecological effects of choupique depletion should be studied.

Sport fishermen usually seek different catches from the ones mentioned above. Perhaps the most popular fish taken for sport are the large-mouth bass and other species of the *Micropterus* genus. Although this fish is extremely popular as a game fish, it is not offered as a specialty in restaurants bordering the Basin, nor is it sold commercially. Another very popular fish with sportsmen is the sacalait, or white crappie (*Poxomis annularis Raf.*). It is possible to make a large *sacalait* catch with rod and reel because of the schooling behavior of this fish. *Sacalait* are a local favorite at fish fries. Other popular schooling fish are the various bream, sunfish, and perch (genus *Lepomis*), which the Cajuns call *patasas*.

Fishing Techniques

Commercial fishermen drifting into the area from the upper Mississippi system introduced many fishing techniques used in the Atchafalaya Basin. One very old technique brought into this region involves the use of a hook and line. Two broad categories of bait—"cut-bait" and "live bait"—are used in conjunction with the hook and line. Cut-bait is usually made by cutting larger fish into pieces. Smaller fish, such

as shad or shiners, as well as small crawfish and river shrimp, are used as live bait. The most common hook-and-line technique used by commercial fishermen involves the use of a trotline. Trotlines are lines from which hooks are hung at close intervals by way of thinner short lines called "stagings." A variety of specialized terms are used for trotlines depending upon the particular manner in which they are used in fishing. Anchor lines, cross lines, string lines, float lines and buoy lines are a few of the variations. These lines are sometimes (illegally) set across a river, bayou, or lake; or they may be strung up in the woods during flood season. Since the invention of nylon twine, which lasts much longer than the original cotton twine, fishermen often leave their trotlines in place year-round. Catfish and gaspergou are the commercial fish most often caught on trotlines.

Hoop nets are also commonly used in the Atchafalaya Basin. They are long cylindrical net traps with one or more funnel-shaped openings sewn onto a framework of rigid hoops. A fish that enters the large end of the funnel and swims through the restriction in the net is unable to escape. Two categories of hoop nets are generally used, large and small. The smaller nets are knotted into 1" - 2" diamond meshes and are used primarily to catch channel catfish. The larger nets, utilizing 4" mesh, are used to catch blue catfish, buffalofish, and gaspergou, while allowing smaller fish to escape. During the spring flood, hoop nets are used in conjunction with a lead net. The lead net, a heavy-lined net that is as high as the diameter of the largest hoop, is attached between two hoop nets. These nets are placed perpendicular to the water current in "roads" cut by the fishermen during low water. As moving fish hit this lead net, they are directed to the hoop nets at either end.

Other fish netting techniques became popular to commercial fishermen in the Basin. Two general types of seines, the "haul" seine, which is pulled to shore; and the "roundup" seine, which is used in the middle of lakes, were once commonly used in the Basin. The gill net, made of a single mesh large enough to permit only the head of the fish to penetrate up to the gills is still fairly popular in some areas of the Basin, as is the trammel net which utilizes three meshes of netting to entrap the fish.

[continued on page 63]

Atchafalaya Basin Boats & Boat Builders*

*Material on pages 55-62 is used courtesy of the Louisiana Folklife Program.
For more information, please visit http://www.louisianafolklife.org/

photo by Malcolm Comeaux.

Here is an old-time Atchafalaya Basin bateau putt-putt. These long bateaux (often 24' long, 3' wide at the bottom) were the most popular fishing and all-purpose vessels in the Basin during the first half of the twentieth century. They were powered by two-cycle, water-cooled, inboard gasoline engines that came in single cylinder (2 hp and 4 hp), and double cylinder (6 hp and 8 hp) models. The Lockwood-Ash company of Michigan first produced these motors prior to World War I, permitting Sears and Roebuck to sell them under the name "Motorgo" as early as 1916. These engines remained in demand in the Atchafalaya Basin long after they were obsolete elsewhere in the country. Nadler Foundry and Machine Company of Plaquemine (Iberville Parish) continued to recondition and machine parts for them into the late 1940s. During the 1950s, these bateaux were fairly rapidly replaced by shorter flat boats powered by outboard motors. In 1969, Malcolm Comeaux reported very few bateaux remaining in the swamp. However, a renewed interest in the bateau, beginning in the mid-1980s, has resulted in many restoration and new construction projects. No longer employed in local fisheries, dozens of these bateaux can be seen at boat shows and boat parades.

photo by Malcolm Comeaux.

These Henderson Lake fishermen are pulling in a roundup seine, also known as a traveling seine. Not used anymore, the traveling seine was unique to lakes of the Atchafalaya swamp. Ranging from 300 to 800 feet in length, traveling seines were attached to a long pole fitted with a traveling wheel which rolled along the lake bottom. A skiff (pictured in foreground) was often used to help deploy this seine, and it was hauled aboard a flat-bottom barge, which provided a stable work surface and adequate capacity for seine, seiners, and catch. Three-person crews were typical: one man pulled in the bottom line, one pulled the cork line, and one removed fish from the seine. The common catch was buffalofish, a species which has declined in value since 1940.

Atchafalaya Basin Boats & Boat Builders

photo by Malcolm Comeaux.

When the photo at top left was taken, Atchafalaya Basin fish-buying boats were no longer in operation. In their heyday, which spanned most of the first half of the twentieth century, fish-buying boats transported the catch of swamp fishermen living in remote camps to commercial processing and shipping docks. Common hauls for these boats consisted of channel catfish (*Ictalurus punctatus*), buffalofish (*Ictiobus cyprinellus*), and gaspergou (*Aplodinotus grunniens*). Built along the lines of early twentieth-century Atchafalaya bateaux, these cypress fish-buying boats were powered by inboard gasoline engines. However, compared to typical bateaux, fish-buying boats were longer (26 ft. or better) and wider (6 ft. or so), and they were fit with cabins, covered weighing decks, and ample hold storage for fish and ice. The need for fish-buying boats diminished during the 1950s as fishermen emigrated from the swamp to dryland communities on the spillway edge. Thereafter, Atchafalaya fishermen used speedier outboard motorized boats for travel to and from fishing grounds and for transporting their own catch to market.

photo by Malcolm Comeaux.

Pirogues built of cypress planks, and eventually marine plywood, replaced dugout pirogues during the twentieth century. In Louisiana, modern plank and plywood pirogues demonstrate regional variation and stylistic peculiarities. Mr. Wiltz's plywood pirogue (bottom, left) represents the typical pirogue of the Henderson area, located on the western fringe of the Atchafalaya Basin. Like most pirogues of this region, this one is fitted with a sort of coaming which runs along the top of the gunwales on each side of the boat. These coaming strips function as "stiffeners" providing structural soundness for a vessel which has no conventional frames (ribs). Distinctive features which set western Atchafalaya Basin pirogues apart from others in Louisiana include coaming strips, thwarts placed across the midsection to form a live-well for bait or fish, and gently curving bow stems.

Atchafalaya Basin Boats & Boat Builders

photo by Malcolm Comeaux.

Here is Mrs. Ann Cavalier rowing her Creole skiff (local French, *esquif*) on Little Grand Bayou near Lake Verret. These skiffs were once common on the eastern fringe of the Atchafalaya Swamp and elsewhere in southeast Louisiana. Notice the yoke (local French, *joug*) which elevates the oars providing greater leverage to forward-facing rowers in a standing position. These skiffs were popular for individual and family travel and transportation, especially on open bayous and lakes, and for fishing, moss gathering, and other swamp exploitations prior to the advent of the gasoline engine. Creole skiffs had become very rare, and localized to the Pierre Part vicinity in Assumption Parish, when this photo was taken in the late 1960s. Since the mid-1980s, there has been a minor revival in the building of these skiffs.

In this image, geographer Malcolm Comeaux examines "the only remaining serviceable pirogue" he could locate in the Atchafalaya basin (*Atchafalaya Swamp Life*, 1972). The pirogue is the oldest boat type in Louisiana, and dugout pirogues remained popular far into the twentieth century. However, due to the increasing market value of cypress logs and to increased availability of sawn planks, plank pirogues began replacing dugouts after the turn of the twentieth century. By 1930, prime cypress logs needed for dugout building were relatively scarce. Changing patterns of boat maintenance and storage also contributed to the demise of the dugout. Cypress dugouts (and other cypress boats, for that matter) are most useful and durable when left floating, or partially submerged, in water. Frequent hauling and relaunching, resulting in cycles of wood-fiber swelling and shrinking, leads to the splitting of cypress hulls. Unfortunately, as the twentieth century progressed, pirogues (and other small boats) were more likely to be stolen if left unattended at water's edge. Modern habits of trailering and relaunching boats were firmly established. These habits adversely affect the durability of wooden boats, generally reducing the viability of wooden boat building traditions in their wake.

photo by Malcolm Comeaux.

Atchafalaya Basin Boats & Boat Builders

photo by Adrian Gauthier.

photo courtesy the Raymond Sedotal family.

Raymond Sedotal (1924-2006) is here (left, top image) seated in his pirogue near his home in Pierre Part. Raymond built a great variety of cypress, cypress and plywood, and aluminum boats. His solidly-built pirogues were, and many still are, used by crawfishermen and other swampers working in the eastern Atchafalaya Basin. Raymond's skills as a timber cutter, wood worker, and boat builder developed in the swamp. At a young age, he went to work with his father at a floating logging camp in the Atchafalaya Basin. Raymond's boats are built of cypress that he himself pulled from the swamp. For years, Raymond supported local wooden boat building traditions by supplying builders with high quality cypress lumber, pre-cut cypress head blocks, and boat ribs. He also supplied tupelo gum blocks for many Louisiana duck decoy carvers.

Treasured in his own community, Raymond's boat building mastery has been acclaimed throughout the state and beyond. In 1983, his notoriety was boosted when he was invited to Washington D. C. to build boats on the National Mall at the Smithsonian's Festival of American Folklife. Raymond was invited to return several times to that Smithsonian event, and he demonstrated his skills at many major festivals in Louisiana, including the 1984 World Exposition, the Louisiana Folklife Festival, New Orleans Jazz and Heritage Festival, Audubon Zoo, Lafayette Native Craft Festival, the Natchitoches Folk Festival, and many others. Raymond's boats have been acquired and displayed by the Smithsonian, Center for Traditional Louisiana Boat Building, Jean Lafitte National Park, and Vermilionville Cajun and Creole Folklife Village.

photo courtesy the Raymond Sedotal family.

Atchafalaya Basin Boats & Boat Builders

Raymond built the Creole skiff seen in both images on this page during public demonstrations at the Folklife Pavilion of the 1984 World's Fair. The Creole skiff was once common on the eastern fringe of the Atchafalaya Swamp, and elsewhere in southeast Louisiana. It has a fish-shaped overhead profile with full bow and finely tapered transom. The sides of a Creole skiff are flared widely, and it has considerable forward sheer. Perhaps its most interesting feature is a yoke (local French, *joug*) fastened athwart at midships which elevates the oars a foot or so above the gunwales. The oars of this skiff are attached with leather straps to tholepins which fit into the joug. This elevated fulcrum permits the oarsman to row standing upright facing forward.

Raymond was assisted in the building of this skiff by his uncle, Alex Giroir. Alex's father, Alexandre Giroir (Raymond's grandfather), was an acknowledged master builder of skiffs in the Pierre Part area early during the twentieth century. As the century progressed, the Creole skiff became all but obsolete and, prior to this 1984 Creole skiff project, a half century had passed since one had been built. Thanks to Raymond Sedotal and Alex Giroir, this beautiful traditional form was saved from the scrap heap of history. After 1984, Raymond was called upon many times to build such skiffs—full-sized and scale models.

photo courtesy of the Louisiana Folklife Program.

In the Fall of 1999, this 1984 World's Fair Creole skiff traveled to the Peabody Essex Museum in Salem, Massachusetts, where it become part of a groundbreaking exhibition entitled "Suggestive Curves." After leaving the Peabody Essex, the Sedotal/Giroir Creole skiff crossed the Atlantic Ocean aboard a freighter to join the 2000 Fêtes Maritimes de Douarnenez (near Brest, France), the most prestigious traditional wooden boat show in the world. Upon return from France, the little skiff rejoined the permanent collection of the Center for Traditional Louisiana Boat Building at Nicholls State University in Thibodaux.

photo courtesy the Raymond Sedotal family.

Atchafalaya Basin Boats & Boat Builders

photo courtesy Jim Delahoussaye.

photo courtesy Jim Delahoussaye.

During the spring and summer of 2006, Edward Couvillier built this 16-ft. outboard-motorized bateau at his current home on the Oxford Loop of Bayou Teche near Franklin. The project was supported by an apprenticeship grant provided by the Louisiana Division of the Arts, Louisiana Folklife Program. Serving as apprentices for this project were Ed's son, Kevin, and his long-time friend, Jim Delahoussaye. Edward's other two sons, Justin and Larry, frequently helped on the project.

This type of bateau was inspired by the older inboard-motorized bateaux putt-putts that dominated the Atchafalaya from around WWI until the early 1950s. With the advent of the outboard motor, builders like Ed Couvillier shortened the length of the older hull design, broadened its transom, and developed a hull designed to plane at higher speeds. Ed used a boat like this for over thirty years as a commercial line fisherman. But, by the end of the 1970s, cypress boat stock had become rare. Alternate building materials and boat forms replaced the wooden bateaux. Today, it is fairly rare to find a wooden boat of any kind in the Atchafalaya area. It is special to find someone who can build a bateau using traditional materials and techniques.

photo courtesy Jim Delahoussaye.

Atchafalaya Basin Boats & Boat Builders

Edward was born in 1928 on Little Bayou Pigeon. He lived on houseboats within the interior of the swamp, moving periodically with his family to places like Catfish Bayou, Keelboat Pass, the Atchafalaya main channel, and Goat Island. Eventually, in 1946, he moved to Myon's Canal, near Myette Point. The next year, he married Lena Mae Bailey, a girl from that community. In 1949, Ed, along with other members of the camp boat village at Myon's Canal, pulled their houseboats over the flood protection levee and settled on the outside apron of the levee. This levee community endured until 1975 when most of the inhabitants moved several miles south to the banks of Bayou Teche at Oxford Loop.

Although Ed and Lena Mae raised their three boys and two girls fishing out of boats very similar to the one on this page, their children had never built a boat like this. This project provided an opportunity for Ed's sons to reconnect with a part of their heritage they had never fully experienced. The Couvillier family is typical of many families from former fishing communities all around the Atchafalaya. During the last half of the twentieth century, these families migrated out of the swamp, leaving dwindling fishing grounds for new land-based occupations and lifestyles. This project proves that some descendants of these displaced swampers can and do maintain the sorts of close ties with elders that permit the continuity of wetland heritage.

photo courtesy Jim Delahoussaye.

photo courtesy Jim Delahoussaye.

Atchafalaya Basin Boats & Boat Builders

Albert (nicknamed Gouyou) Latiolais (d. 1993) is seen (top, right) motoring along in his bateau putt-putt, near his home in Henderson. Albert was born and raised in Happy Town, an extinct community once located on the west bank of the Atchafalaya River above Butte LaRose. His love for wood working was influenced by his father, Lionel Latiolais, a fisherman, boat builder, and carpenter who moved his family to Henderson during the 1940s. Albert became a master builder of local traditional fishing craft, designing and building outboard-motorized flat boats of exceptional performance and quality. He also developed a type of wooden hydroplane racing boat that became famous in local races, and he built competition racing dugouts which he occasionally paddled in the Lafitte pirogue races.

Along with his brothers Tony and Darrell, Albert was invited to demonstrate boat building skills at the 1985 Smithsonian Festival of American Folklife. The bateau pictured in this image was built on the National Mall in Washington, D.C. Bateaux of this type were very popular in the Atchafalaya Basin throughout the first half of the twentieth century. They were used for a wide range of fishing activities, but also provided basic travel and transport for many swamp families in the Atchafalaya. Well over 20 ft. in length, these cypress displacement hulls were powered by early-twentieth century single- or double-cylinder inboard gasoline motors. The peculiar sound of these early gasoline engines inspired the boat's local name: "bateau putt-putt."

(Bottom, right) Alcide Verret paddles his pirogue in the Atchafalaya Basin, St. Martin Parish. By the late 1940s, after high flood protection levees confined the Atchafalaya Basin, and after most swampers had resettled on dry ground outside of the protective levees, a handful of people refused to leave the swamp. Alcide Verret (b. 12/29/1902, d. 9/26/1996) chose to stay. Born in the swamp, Verret made his home on Bayou Sorrell, near the Main Channel of the Atchafalaya, where he continued to fish, crawfish, and live in general harmony with the swamp for nearly the entire twentieth century. In a forested swamp virtually devoid of dryland roads, the pirogue demonstrates its value. A single boatman with a pirogue can negotiate shallow stump-filled waters, portage easily when needed, paddle swiftly over considerable distances, and tend to much of the work of a swamper: running fishing lines, following wetland game trails, gliding up silently on fat frogs, and so forth.

photo by Adrian Gauthier.

photo by Calvin Voisin.

[continued from page 54]

Having witnessed drastic changes in this category, the fishing industry is still rapidly changing. Twentieth century inventions like the outboard motor and nylon twine have made fishing easier than ever before. Artificial waterways, new channel cutoffs, pipeline canals, borrow pit canals, etc., allow fishermen to reach parts of the Basin that were difficult or impossible to reach before. Twentieth century changes are not without costs. Erratic control of the water level in parts of the Basin often causes fish to suffocate from loss of oxygen. Chemicals washing into the Basin waters from surrounding agricultural land can result in fish kills. Waste from oil drilling wells extracts an incalculable toll from the fish industry. Most dangerous of all is the progressing siltation of the Basin. As the Basin gradually filled with sediment, commercial fishermen were forced increasingly southward toward Morgan City. Eventually, the once huge Grand Lake was nearly completely filled with sediment. Much of one of the world's most productive fishing grounds has been lost—along with the livelihood of many Atchafalaya fishing families.

Boat Types

A variety of water craft was used in the swamp. Dugout pirogues, sculpted from cypress logs, became essential to Atchafalaya swamp life. These dugouts were eventually replaced by cypress-plank pirogues, built in various styles according to distinct local traditions. Newer versions using marine plywood replaced the plank boats when cypress became scarce. Keeping pace with the times, now most pirogues are built of fiberglass or aluminum. Pirogues are propelled by paddle, usually operated by a single individual. They are particularly useful in shallow and stump-infested waters.

A flat-bottomed boat with blunt bow and stern provided the basic form from which many work boats developed. *Chaland* is the ancient French term for a flatboat—a term still used by the older generation. *Chalands* were modified in shape and size for many uses: line and/or net fishing, moss-gathering, local ferry transport, etc. Larger versions, often called barges, were built for heavy hauling and transportation. Similar barges provided flotation for houseboats. The generalized *chaland* form was elongated and motorized to become the Atchafalaya Basin bateau putt-putt, the most popular all-around boat used by Atchafalaya residents during the first half of the twentieth century. These were powered by inboard gasoline engines. A rise in popularity of outboard motors in the 1950s led to the rapid decline of the bateau putt-putts. They were replaced by a shorter, wooden-hull bateau designed to plane on the water at much higher speeds. Wooden bateaux are rare today; aluminum-hull boats have replaced them.

Many varieties of skiffs have been built in the Basin. Specifically boats with blunt sterns and pointed bows. The French term for this boat is *esquif*. Among these, the Creole skiff, a boat propelled by a standing, forward-facing oarsman, has been widely recognized for its distinctive beauty and its important contribution to Louisiana French heritage. These Creole skiffs are very rare today, but a pair of them can be seen at Vermilionville, the Cajun/Creole folklife attraction in Lafayette. Raymond Sedotal (d. 7/15/2006), master boat builder from Pierre Part, constructed them around 1990. Aluminum skiffs dominate the Basin today and many are custom-built by superb craftsmen.

Crawfishing

Though crawfish have been eaten in Louisiana since before European arrival, the crawfish industry in the Atchafalaya Basin did not start until the early 1950s. This late start resulted from insufficient means of storing crawfish. Before the invention of the icebox and rapid transportation, crawfish was a seasonal delicacy enjoyed only by the swamp dwellers. Since the 1950s, however, crawfishing has become one of the most profitable industries in the Basin. Twenty years ago, the estimated average annual commercial harvest of Atchafalaya Basin crawfish was around twenty-two million pounds. This haul provided substantial incomes to quite a few Cajuns. Before the proliferation of farm-raised crawfish, and depending on their fluctuating market value, many inhabitants living on the fringes of the Basin would quit good-paying jobs during crawfish season to devote all of their energies to the industry.

A variety of specialized gear has been developed by the Basin crawfisherman. The boat he use is most often flat-bottomed with a pointed bow and a blunt stern. This pointed bow allows the crawfisherman to go through water hyacinths as well as navigate more easily in heavily wooded swamps. The steering mechanism of these boats is often placed in the bow section to allow easier swamp navigation. Although wooden boats dominated the industry for years, virtually all crawfishermen now utilize aluminum boats. The typical crawfish trap is cylindrical with a funnel on one end with a clasp to open the other end when removing the catch. Initially made of chicken wire, these traps are now made locally with specialized steel. Several hundred of these traps may be used by a single crawfisherman. Crawfish traps are usually baited with shad or various sorts of cut bait; however, pelletized bait made of grain and fish oil is also used.

The modern crawfisherman has adapted his technique to special conditions offered by the Spillway environment. The annual flood within the Spillway provides the necessary biological requirements for crawfish better than any other area of the state. When the spring water begins to rise in the Basin, the crawfisherman launches his boat from a ramp built on the side of the artificial flood protection levee. He often guides his custom-made aluminum boat through a deep-water forested swamp that is dry to boggy forestland most of the year.

Unfortunately for the crawfisherman, recent environmental conditions seem to be changing rapidly for the worst. In many places in the swamp, each flood deposits a layer of sand on good crawfish-breeding soils. In some places, crawfish habitats are destroyed by a lack of free flowing water. Man-made levees and dredge piles often trap stagnant backwater, robbing it of sufficient oxygen for crawfish production. Some crawfishermen are calling for increased water supply in the Basin, and removal of water flow obstructions. Meanwhile, the annual harvest of wild Atchafalaya crawfish has dropped by half or more during the past several years.

Recently, wild crawfish production also is in decline because of market challenges. Beginning in the 1960s, a boom in artificial crawfish farms has cut deeply into the wild crawfish market. And, within the

Shallow draft dugout pirogues like this were often used for hunting and fishing in the Basin. (Andrew Lytle, photographer; courtesy of the Louisiana and Lower Mississippi Valley Collection, Louisiana State University Library.)

last two decades, globalizing market forces have created a situation wherein imported crawfish from Asia undercuts the price of Louisiana produced crawfish of any kind. Restaurants and retail grocers often turn to cheaper imports and away from the local catch. In addition to the destructive influence of Chinese crawfish on the local market, Hurricane Katrina had the effect of greatly reducing the size of the New Orleans market's demand for live and peeled crawfish.

Crabbing

The crab industry in the Basin began commercially in the Morgan City area around 1920. The most effective technique used by crabbers employs a baited trotline often a mile or more in length. As the crabber runs his boat along the trotline, the line passes over a roller mounted to the boat by an outrigger. This roller lifts the line out of the water, allowing the crabber to scoop the crabs off the baited line with a shallow net while operating the boat with his other hand. Cylindrical or square heavy-wire traps are also used, though they are not as efficient as the trotline method.

Both crabbing and processing are still concentrated around Morgan City. The crabs are transported to a processing facility that cooks and peels the crabs and packages the meat for distribution. Large crab processing plants have recently opened in the Henderson area. Crabs are usually trucked north to Henderson, where the processing often is accomplished by Vietnamese.

The crab industry has been damaged to some degree by physiographic changes taking place in the Basin. When the flood protection levees were originally built during the 1930s, many good crabbing areas were destroyed. Catahoula Lake, Lake Fausse Pointe, Lake Verret, and Pierre Part Bay are a few spots outside the flood levees that were adversely affected. Now, as the great Basin lakes fill with sediment, crab production is lessening within the Spillway confines. As can be said about fishing and crawfishing, crabbing is rapidly becoming an endangered profession.

Frogging

The Louisiana bullfrog (*Rana catesbeiana*) and the Southern bullfrog (*Rana grylio*), both called *ouaouaron* by French speakers of Louisiana, are gathered in great numbers from the Basin. The commercial frog industry developed during the late 1800s and was centered in Morgan City at the head of the Southern Pacific Rail line. In recent years, frog production has declined in the state because of the destruction of suitable habitats by drainage, flood control measures, and other such activities of man. These developments have adversely affected frog production in the Basin also, though the Spillway today offers the best remaining environment for the propagation of frogs in the state. Frogs are generally taken at night with the aid of some type of artificial light. The light renders the frogs' eyes luminous as well as immobilizing the creatures, making their capture possible. Often the frogger makes his catch by hand while walking in the water near the bank or from a boat. A variety of gigs and nets are also employed for the purpose. The spear gig, once a popular frogging device, is now outlawed in Louisiana. The "grab gig," a device which allows frogs to be taken alive (theoretically, at least) is often used. A small net attached to the end of a long pole is occasionally used with success.

Trapping

Exploitation of fur-bearing animals has been an important industry within the Basin since the advent of white habitation. Before the 1950s, the muskrat (*Ondatra zibethicus rivalicius*) was the most numerous catch. Since that time, the nutria (*Myocastor coypus*), pronounced "neutral" by many swamp and marsh inhabitants, has become most important. Mink (*Mustela vison vilgivaga*), raccoon (*Procyon lotor lotor*), otter (*Lutra canadensis*), beaver (*Castor canadensis*), striped skunk (*Mephitis mephitis*) , opossum (*Didelphis virginiana*), red fox (*Vulpes fulva*), gray fox (*Urocyon cinereoargenteus*), and coyote (*Canis latrans*) are all exploited for their fur (see Lowery, 1974).

Human modification of the Basin has affected the trapping industry. Because of the large number of man-made canals, most trapping today is done from a boat along shorelines, whereas placing traps along a walked line was once the only way to exploit many areas. The extreme variation in Spillway water level is not ideal for fur production. For this reason, trapping in the Basin never matched the significance of fur production in the coastal marshes. These issues aside, a growing anti-fur coalition has succeeded in demolishing the fur industry in Louisiana and elsewhere during the past several decades.

Turtle Industry

A commercial turtle industry began in the Basin around 1900. The common snapping turtle (*Chelydra serpentina serpentina*) and the alligator snapping turtle (*Macrochelys temminckii*), are both commercially exploited today. Turtles are taken in various ways, depending upon the season. During the summer, they are sometimes caught on baited line, but the most common method employs the hoop net. Hoop nets are baited with fresh meat and placed along the shore with at least part of the net above water. If the net is placed completely under the water, the entrapped turtle will drown or break the net trying to get oxygen. During the winter, while turtles are hibernating beneath the ground surface, swampers locate them by probing with a heavy iron rod. The rod has a large hook which allows the turtle to be pulled out once it is located.

Along with the two types of snapping turtles, the softshell turtle (*Trionyx muticus*) is also locally prized for its meat. Many restaurants around the Atchafalaya Basin, especially those near Pierre Part, specialize in turtle dishes. The demand for turtle meat has prompted some businessmen to establish artificial turtle ponds.

Alligator Industry

The alligator (*Alligator mississippiensis*) has been prized by swamp dwellers since before European contact for various reasons. Indians (and later many other swampers) took alligators for their edible flesh and oil that could be used for medicinal purposes. The oil also was used historically in the processing of indigo, and later as a lubricant for steam engines.

The most important product obtained from alligators, however, has always been hides. Various fads which required alligator hides for shoes, boots, belts, hatbands, etc., resulted in great slaughter of these animals. As a result of these depredations, alligator populations

A "major" alligator catch. (From *Century Magazine*, 1892)

declined drastically and extinction of the species seemed eminent. It was not until the 1960s that alligators became legally protected in Louisiana. Since that time, the population has increased greatly; in fact, they have become nuisances in some regions. For this reason, a limited hunting season for alligator was opened, beginning during the late 1970s, as a population management measure. When the official alligator-hunting season was first re-established, alligators were hunted mainly for their skin. Often the meat of the skinned alligator was thrown away. Before long, hunters began to better realize the value of their catch and sell the meat for 50¢-$3.00 per pound.

Most alligators are caught on a baited line. Rotted meat or fish is attached to a large hook, often a treble hook, which is suspended above the water surface from a pole secured to the bank. Another way of hunting these reptiles is to shoot them at night. The alligator, being a nocturnal creature, is easily hunted with an artificial light that serves to temporarily immobilize them. Today, a great number of alligators are raised on commercial farms. Alligator meat has become a specialty in many restaurants in the Atchafalaya area. Alligator skulls, teeth, claws, paws, and entire stuffed carcasses are available for the tourist trade.

South Louisiana alligator hunter. (Courtesy of the State Library of Louisiana.)

Hunting

Though it has not been commercially important since the early 1900s, hunting has always been an important activity in the Basin. A variety of game resides in this great semi-wilderness expanse, and traditions that pre-date European arrival urge hunters to take advantage of it.

White-tailed deer (*Odocoileus virginianus*) hunting is a favorite of many. The deer is hunted in a variety of manners, some of which are legal. Perhaps the most effective way, though quite illegal, involves shooting the deer at night from a boat or car. The deer are also effectively hunted from a still-stand placed in a tree. These tree-stands often overlook artificial deer-runs such as pipeline crossings, power line rights-of-way, or a variety of roads cut through the thick brush. Others overlook dried up natural streambeds that usually offer excellent conditions as deer paths.

A variety of small game hunting is also practiced. The eastern cottontail (*Sylvilagus floridanus*) and the swamp rabbit (*Sylvilagus aquaticus*), both referred to as "lapin" by French hunters, are regularly sought. The grey squirrel (*Sciurus carolinensis*) and the fox squirrel (*Sciurus niger*) are also popular game. These small game are often hunted with dogs, occasionally taken illegally at night, and otherwise hunted according to the special features offered by the particular hunting grounds. Bird hunting, especially waterfowl, is another important activity.

A variety of migratory fowl—ducks and especially wood ducks, mallards, and several varieties of geese—are hunted in their particular habitats. Wading waterfowl are sometimes hunted, though illegally. Locally called *bec-croche* and *gros-bec* by the French inhabitants, the white ibis (*Eudocimus albus*) and the night heron (*Nycticorax nycticorax*) are prized for their tasty flesh. These birds are also considered competitors by many locals because of their insatiable appetite for crawfish. Upland game birds such as the snipe, quail, dove, woodcock, and occasionally even robin and blackbird are also hunted, both with and without the help of dogs.

A South Louisiana hunting camp, circa 1895. (Image # 10936, Courtesy of the Martin Photo Collection at the Iberia Parish Library in New Iberia.)

Hunters in the Atchafalaya Basin fall into one of two categories. The first is a very select group that either owns land in the Spillway or has the connections and/or money to lease Basin lands. These hunters may or may not live near the Basin, but are usually fairly well endowed financially. In some spots, as around the Pierre Part/Bayou Pigeon area, local inhabitants have organized to form exclusive hunting clubs in order to protect their hunting privileges from outsiders. The second category of Basin hunters is composed of poachers. These are usually local inhabitants of the Basin fringe who know the area well. They go in and out of the swamp, not always during hunting season, without detection. Many feel that their access to hunting areas should at least be equal to the large landowners and wealthy outsiders. Many poachers do not have the financial resources or political connections to hunt legally, but this does not prevent them from exploiting the abundant wild game of the Basin.

Physiographic changes in the Basin have resulted in both good and bad effects on hunting. The rapid sedimentation in the Basin has created land such that squirrels may be hunted where hoop nets were once set. But, as sedimentation increases, the swamp habitat is increasing at the expense of the natural levee habitats that once existed. This natural levee habitat, complete with edible herbs, vegetables, young shoots, ripening weeds and grass seeds, acorns, nuts, and various fruits, supports one of the richest biotic communities in the Basin. With loss of optimal habitats, the production of game can only decline.

Bee Industry

By the turn of the twentieth century beekeeping had developed in several areas within the Basin. Before the flood protection levees were constructed, hives were kept on platforms raised above the water by posts, or on floating honey barges. Since the building of the levees, most of the hives have been removed from the interior of the Spillway. A thriving apiary industry presently uses the flood protection levees for hive location. This location was originally selected by mutual agreement between local beekeepers and the U.S. Army Corps of Engineers. When the levees were first built, the bees were needed to help pollinate the newly planted clover, placed there to prevent erosion of levee material. The beekeepers, needing a dry place to put their hives, consented to locating on the artificial levee. Since then, the willow swamps on the interior of the artificial levees have become an ample collecting ground for bees.

Moss Industry

Commercial gathering of Spanish moss began in the Basin sometime during the latter part of the nineteenth century. Moss was used, in its cured form, for anything that needed stuffing: mattresses, chairs, saddles, car seats, and horse collars. Moss production hit a peak in the 1930s. The gathering of moss was the only way to earn a living by many swampers of those Depression years. It was during this decade that the older methods of hand curing and ginning moss gave way to more modern, efficient methods, some of which were derived from the cotton industry.

After the Depression, moss production declined gradually until it ceased altogether in 1961. The development of substitutes for the moss, particularly the invention of foam rubber, contributed to the decline of the industry. A few years ago, the industry began to experience a minor revival. A growing demand for moss by the fish hatchery industry, which uses moss as a host for the deposition of roe, has led to this upsurge. But factors of the Basin ecological system now threaten to permanently exterminate the moss industry. When Malcolm Comeaux wrote his excellent treatise of the Atchafalaya Basin (1972), he remarked that, "moss today is abundant because of the lack of recent exploitation." This is no longer true. Within the last decades, Spanish moss has become increasingly hard to find. Informants from many areas of the Basin attest, often with great emotion, to a rapid decline or total disappearance of the once-common epiphyte. Informants offer two hypotheses concerning this recent perdition; either air pollution from surrounding industrial complexes has killed the moss, or the

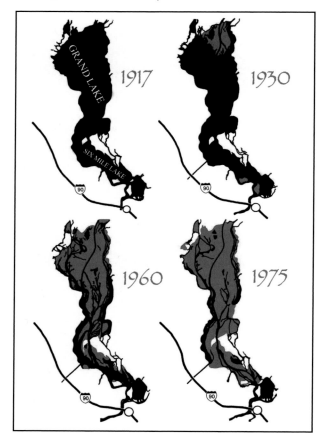

Sediment buildup in some parts of the Basin, as seen here at Grand and Six Mile lakes, is threatening traditional lifestyles and livelihoods. Purple represents sediment accumulation. (From "Evaluation of Sand-Dominant Subaerial Phase, Atchafalaya Delta, Louisiana," by H.H. Roberts, R D. Adams, and R.H.W. Cunningham; *American Association of Petroleum Geology Bulletin*, 1980.)

aerial spraying of herbicides over neighboring agricultural lands has been the cause. Whatever the causal factors, the once-familiar moss-covered landscape of the Atchafalaya Basin is no longer so common.

Modern Spillway to Heritage Area

As we have seen, lifeways and the arrangement of human living space in the Atchafalaya Basin have changed dynamically over the years, in accordance with major changes in natural and social environments. The high water of 1927 marked a great change in Basin settlement patterns.

Prior to the flood, a few thriving villages had sprung up in the interior of the Basin. These included the older established communities of Bayou Chene and Butte LaRose, both of which were established prior to 1850 along important water routes within the swamp. And there were newer villages like Achafalaya Station and Pelba Station that were built on pilings at stops along the Southern Pacific Railroad connecting Baton Rouge and Lafayette. Service on this branch began in 1911, during the heyday of commercial fishing in the Basin. Atchafalaya and Pelba were collecting points for the marketing of fish and other swamp produce. In addition to these, there were dozens of campboat villages scattered throughout the swamp. Some of these villages were more or less permanent and their inhabitants tended to move around seasonally. Lifestyles focused upon seasonal resource exploitation tended to be at least semi-nomadic.

All of this began to change in 1927. The flood was so devastating as to be dangerous even to houseboat owners. One elderly lady from the Bayou Chene community remembered that the flood hit so rapidly that there was no time to untie the line that held her houseboat to the shore. As the water rose dangerously, the line had to be chopped with an axe in order to keep the boat from capsizing. Many dire tragedies accompanied this event. The awesome flood left permanent psycho-logical marks on many, if not all, of those who experienced it. Most surviving residents of the heart of the swamp decided to permanently leave for higher ground.

In the years following the 1927 flood, the Atchafalaya Basin was transformed into the Atchafalaya Spillway. Flood protection levee projects and dredging operations employed many former swamp dwellers. Communities along the fringe of the swamp grew from an influx of levee workers and continued to grow as former swamp dwellers left the swamp interior. This migration was largely completed in the 1950s, leaving only a few individuals and families behind.

Many swampers, still intent on exploiting the Basin, contributed to a peculiar variety of settlement forms on or near the levees. Communities such as Bayou Benoit, Grand Bayou, Little Pass, Myette Point, and many others sprang up directly upon the newly built levees. Often houseboats, once used to inhabit the deep swamp, were hauled on land to make these levee communities. A variety of simple wood frame houses and mobile homes were eventually added to these communities that were shaped to correspond with the linear Spillway levees. Responding to the pleas of relocated residents, boat ramps were constructed on the interior of the levees to allow access to the Basin. The levees themselves offered transportation routes between these communities and the boat ramps.

Increasingly, many inhabitants of the Spillway fringe turned away from the Basin to find outside employment. Many found work in the oilfields, both onshore and in the Gulf. Others found employment at industrial plants, at factories surrounding the Basin, in local agricultural activities, or at a variety of jobs in larger nearby towns. Yet, many retain a camp near the Basin in order to exploit, at least part-time, the many resources offered by the swamp and for recreation.

Following the resettlement of swamp dwellers to the fringes of the Basin, a certain number of former Basin residents continued to focus upon the swamp for their livelihoods, although often supplementing their income with occasional wage-earning jobs. Large-scale commercial crawfishing in the Basin began to develop during the 1950s, and continues to provide an important livelihood for some Cajuns, as does hoopnet fishing and crabbing. Many Cajuns were employed in the construction of Floodway levees and drainage features. Enhancements in waterborne transport and navigation during the past sixty years have provided job opportunities in towboat operation and fabrication. Some jobs in the Basin area are directly or indirectly associated with the oil industry. However, since the availability of oil field-related jobs has proven erratic and unreliable, many locals continue to rely upon the natural resources of the Basin to supplement their economies.

Within the last fifty years, many seafood restaurants and some Cajun dancehalls have sprung up along the fringes of the Basin. Pat's Fisherman's Wharf in Henderson and Mulate's Cajun Restaurant in Breaux Bridge are two longtime famous attractions started by Cajuns who grew up in the Atchafalaya Basin. More recently, there has been a flourish of business activity around the Basin designed to take advantage of tourists' desire to see the swamp and experience Cajun life. For example, the following "Cajun" attractions are currently located within a two-mile strip of levee in Henderson: de la Houssaye's Atchafalaya Expedition Swamp Tours; Cypress Cove Landing Houseboat Adventures; Atchafalaya Basin Landing and Marina; Whiskey River Landing and Club; and McGee's Landing Atchafalaya Basin Swamp Tours. In addition to swamp access, these facilities tend to offer dining facilities, souvenirs, bars, and dance music. Entrepreneurial efforts in Cajun cultural tourism, encouraged by the growing popularity of Cajun cooking and music, are common throughout the region.

We should note that the Atchafalaya area is culturally affected by developments within the larger Acadiana region of south-central and southwest Louisiana. Within the last thirty years there has been an amazing revitalization of cultural expression in this region, sometimes referred to as the Cajun Renaissance. By the early 1960s, interest in local traditional music, the local French language, and other features of local heritage had waned among younger generations. The dominance of national and international pop cultural trends threatened to render the distinctiveness of this area into homogenized American sameness. The work of folklorists, music producers, festival organizers, musicians, and other culture leaders reversed this trend. An amazing and unprecedented rise in popularity of Cajun and Zydeco music, local food, and expressive art began to flourish both inside and outside of Louisiana. This revival began during the early-to-mid-1970s and appears to carry forth unabated. Today, the music of a younger generation of superb musicians invigorates the local music scene at festival venues, local restaurants, and dancehalls.

In spite of this overwhelming cultural revitalization, questions concerning cultural continuity still revolve around language retention. The

Magee's Landing, which operates Atchafalaya Basin Swamp Tours and a popular cafe and bar.

oral French language spoken by Cajuns and Creoles, which includes a range of distinctive local variation, was dominant in many communities in south Louisiana at the turn of the twentieth century. Mandatory English-language education in Louisiana, which began around 1916, severely altered this situation. Cajun and Creole children were punished for speaking French on the school grounds and those who spoke no English, or who spoke with a heavy accent, were often ridiculed and held as the butt of jokes. The powerful stigma that developed among native speakers of French discouraged many parents from teaching French to their offspring. In 1968, the Council for the Development of French in Louisiana (CODOFIL) was established to help salvage a dying language. Its activities, particularly with regard to the promotion of Cajun music, contributed to the current cultural revitalization, but the fate of Louisiana French language is far from secure. Within the last several years, several south Louisiana public schools have initiated French language immersion curriculums. This approach has attained local popularity and considerable success but its availability to Cajun children is limited and unevenly distributed. A number of successful French immersion programs are currently conducted within schools located on the fringes of the Atchafalaya Basin.

Lately, a promising regional tourism development called the Atchafalaya Trace Heritage Area is unfolding. In 2002, the Atchafalaya Trace Commission produced a document titled *The Atchafalaya Trace Heritage Area Management Plan Executive Summary*. This document outlines the goals and strategies of a cultural tourism project aimed at preserving local heritage and traditional enterprises. This initiative seeks to promote economic development for small-scale businesses that show sensitivity to environmental and cultural heritage. It encourages projects that promote economic, social, and environmental sustainability. The Atchafalaya Trace Program, sponsored by the National Park Service, encourages partnership between residents and thirteen Louisiana parishes that border the Basin. At the heart of this project is an appreciation and celebration of the cultural vibrancy and resourcefulness endemic to the folk of this area.

On other fronts, the Atchafalaya Program of the Louisiana Department of Natural Resources has been busy over the last several decades in support of projects aimed at environmental stewardship and recreational improvement. Since 1999, the Atchafalaya Program has been engaged in the management of a fifteen-year program with $85 million of funding provided by Act 920 of the Louisiana Legislature. This initiative develops improvements in the areas of access, public easement, water management, and recreation. Local commercial fishermen as well as a wide range of sports fishermen and recreational boaters all benefit from refurbished and newly-built boat ramps. Water management projects at Bayou Eugene, Schwing Chute, Bayou Postillion, and Buffalo Cove indicate this program's commitment to the improvement of water quality in the Basin. In addition to boat ramps, the Atchafalaya Program has developed welcome centers, public art murals, RV sites, parks, campsites, canoe paddling trails, bird watching sites, and a number of annual educational and recreational events.

Of course, new developments in cultural tourism, initiatives in environmental stewardship, new recreational opportunities, and so forth, must be placed within the context of long-term dynamic change. During the twentieth century, huge sections of the Atchafalaya swamp were filled in with sedimentation. The once awe-inspiring Grand Lake, for example, that occupied approximately 175 square miles of the lower Basin, was nearly completely filled with sand and silt—a willow forest grows there now. The great productive potential for fish, crabs, and crawfish will never occur again in the Atchafalaya (unless, of course, the Mississippi finally decides to come down that way). As a result of great environmental changes in the Atchafalaya, many traditional swamp occupations have either dwindled or disappeared. The great cypress timber has been removed. The great fishing grounds are no longer. Current and future generations of Basin residents will not participate to the same degree in the traditional occupations of their ancestors. Still, there are many who work and play in the swamp, and many who carry forth deep traditional knowledge about that environment and its resources. And there are many more who deeply respect the heritage of the Basin, and enjoy the *joie de vivre* of its residents. It is up to us, then, as inheritors of the Atchafalaya, to conserve its environment and heritage as best we can. For our generation and those that follow, it will remain one of the most beautiful and fascinating cultural landscapes we can visit.

Suggestions for Further Reading

Abbey, Gail D. *Life in the Atchafalaya Swamp*. Lafayette, La.: Lafayette Natural History Museum, 1979.

Barry, John M. *Rising Tide: The Great Mississippi Flood of 1927 and How It Changed America*. New York: Simon & Schuster, 1997.

Bergeron, Maida Owens. "Language Maintenance and Shift in a Bayou Community: Four Mile Bayou, near Lake Verret." M.A. thesis, Louisiana State University, 1978.

Brassieur, C. Ray. "The Atchafalaya Basin" in *Mississippi Delta Ethnographic Overview*, edited by Nicholas R. Spitzer. New Orleans: Jean Lafitte National Historical Park and Preserve, 1979.

_____. "Bateau Fait à la Main: Public Boat Building and Waterborne Tourism in Louisiana." *Practicing Anthropology* 27:4 (Fall 2005).

_____. "Louisiana Boatbuilding: An Unfathomed Fortune" in *Louisiana Folklife Festival Program*. Baton Rouge: Louisiana Department of Culture, Recreation, and Tourism, 1989.

Case, Gladys C. *The Bayou Chene Story: A History of the Atchafalaya Basin and Its People*. Detroit: Harlo Press, 1973.

Comeaux, Malcolm. *Atchafalaya Swamp Life: Settlement and Folk Occupations*. Baton Rouge: School of Geoscience, Louisiana State University, 1972.

_____. "Louisiana's Acadians: The Environmental Impact." In *The Cajuns: Essays on Their History and Culture*, edited by Glenn R. Conrad. Lafayette: Center for Louisiana Studies, University of Southwestern Louisiana, 1978.

Conrad, Glenn R. and Carl A. Brasseaux. *Crevasse! The 1927 Flood in Acadiana*. Lafayette: Center for Louisiana Studies, University of Southwestern Louisiana, 1994.

Delcambre, Kenneth P. *Lords of the Basin: History of the Lost Village . . . Atchafalaya, Louisiana*. Henderson, La.: Kenneth P. Delcambre, 1988.

Edwards, Jay D. *Louisiana's Remarkable French Vernacular Architecture*. The Fred B. Kniffen Cultural Resources Laboratory Monograph Series. Baton Rouge: Geoscience Publications, 1988.

Esman, Marjorie R. *Henderson, Louisiana: Cultural Adaptation in a Cajun Community*. New York: Holt, Rinehart and Winston, 1985.

Gatschet, Albert S. "Chitimacha." *Bulletin of the Bureau of American Ethnology* 30:1 (1907).

_____. "The Shetimasha Indians of St. Mary's Parish, Southern Louisiana." *Transactions of the Anthropological Society of Washington* 2 (1882): 148-158.

Gibson, Jon L. *Archaeological Survey of the Lower Atchafalaya Region, South Central Louisiana, Report No. 5*. Lafayette: Center for Archaeological Studies, University of Southwestern Louisiana, 1978.

Goodwin, R. Christopher, Jill-Karen Yakubik, Galloway W. Shelby, Kenneth R. Jones, Debra Stayner, and Janice Cooper. *An Archaeological and Sites Inventory of Bayou Teche between Franklin and Jeanerette, Louisiana*. Baton Rouge: Division of Archaeology, Louisiana State Department of Culture, Recreation and Tourism.

Guirard, Greg. *Atchafalaya Autumn*. St. Martinville, La., 1995.

_____. *Cajun Families of the Atchafalaya/Les familles 'cadien de l'Atchafalaya*. St. Martinville, La., 1989; revised and expanded, 1999.

_____. *The Land of Dead Giants/La royaume des géants morts*. St. Martinville, La., 1991; English and French edition, 2001.

_____. *Seasons of Light in the Atchafalaya Basin*. St. Martinville, La., 1983.

Hoover, Herbert. *The Chitimacha People*. Phoenix, Az.: Indian Tribal Series, 1975.

Suggestions for Further Reading

King, Peggy Elaine. "The Effects of Displacement on Levee Dwellers, Atchafalaya Basin, La." M.A. thesis, Louisiana State University, 1977.

Kniffen, Fred B. "The Indian Mounds of Iberville Parish" in *Reports on the Geology of Iberville and Ascension Parishes*. Louisiana Geological Survey, Bulletin No. 13, 1938.

Kniffen, Fred B. and Malcolm Comeaux. "The Spanish Moss Industry of Louisiana," *Melanges* 12. Baton Rouge: Louisiana State University School of Geoscience, 1979.

Kniffen, Fred B., Hiram F. Gregory, and George A. Stokes. *The Historic Indian Tribes of Louisiana from 1542 to the Present*. Baton Rouge: Louisiana State University Press, 1987.

Knipmeyer, William B. *A Culturo-Geographic Analysis of the Bayou Settlements of Southeastern Louisiana*. Baton Rouge, La.: US Office of Naval Research, 1962.

_____. "Folk Boats of Eastern French Louisiana." In *American Folklife*, edited by Don Yoder. Austin: University of Texas, 1976.

Lockwood, C.C. *Atchafalaya: America's Largest River Basin Swamp*. Baton Rouge: Beauregard Press, 1981.

Mancil, Ervin. "An Historical Geography of Industrial Cypress Lumbering in Louisiana." Ph.D. dissertation, Louisiana State University, 1972.

McFee, John. "The Control of Nature: Atchafalaya." *The New Yorker 63* (February 23, 1987).

_____. *The Control of Nature*. New York: Farrar, Straus & Giroux, 1989.

Norgress, Rachael E. "History of the Cypress Industry in Louisiana." *Louisiana Historical Quarterly 30* (1947): 979-1059.

Rees, Mark A. "Plaquemine Mounds of the Western Atchafalaya Basin." In *Plaquemine Archaeology*, edited by Mark A. Rees and Patrick C. Livingood. Tuscaloosa: University of Alabama Press, 2007.

Reuss, Martin. *Designing the Bayous: The Control of Water in the Atchafalaya Basin, 1800-1995*. College Station: Texas A&M University Press, 2004.

Spitzer, Nicholas R. "Black Creoles of Louisiana." In *Encyclopedia of World Cultures, Volume I, North America*, edited by Timothy J. O'Leary and David Levinson. Boston: G.K. Hall & Co. 1991.

Spitzer, Nicholas R., ed. *Louisiana Folklife: A Guide to the State*. Baton Rouge, Department of Culture, Recreation, and Tourism, 1985.

_____. *Mississippi Delta Ethnographic Overview*. Prepared for the NPS by the National Council for the Traditional Arts. New Orleans: Jean Lafitte National Historical Park and Preserve, 1979.

Swanton, John R. *The Indians of the Southeastern United States*. Bureau of American Ethnology Bulletin 137 (1946).

_____. *Indian Tribes of the Lower Mississippi Valley and Adjacent Coast of the Gulf of Mexico*. Bureau of American Ethnology Bulletin 43 (1911).

_____. *A Structural and Lexical Comparison of the Tunica, Chitimacha, and Atakapa Languages*. Bureau of American Ethnology Bulletin 68 (1919).

White, R.M. *"Cultural Gumbo?": An Ethnographic Overview of Louisiana's Mississippi River Delta*. A Report Prepared for Jean Lafitte National Historical Park and Preserve, 1998.

The photographer on one of his frequent visits to the home of Harold and Myrtle Bigler, 1987. (Photo courtesy of Philip Gould.)

Preserving the Inheritance:

A Photographic Essay with Interviews & Comments

by

Greg Guirard

I took this photograph of a great egret at Bayou Benoit in September 1980. It was on the cover of my first book and twenty-six years after it was originally taken, it is still my favorite image of the swamp.

Cypress trees covered with Spanish moss stand among beds of American lotus at Sandy Cove – summer 1996.

A pair of one-pound blue crabs caught in the main channel of the Atchafalaya - August or September, 1995.

A crate of blue crabs caught in Lake Dauterive - about 1990.

I have my favorite places in the Atchafalaya Basin, and I take refuge in them over and over. I believe that I may see and understand more by spending 30 or 40 days and nights in one or two of these places than by spending the same amount of time in 30 or 40 different swamps. There's something about being out in the swamp, especially when you're alone, that seems to suck the poisons of civilization out of you—some sort of healing power in the air, the fog, the woods and waters, the tranquility, that melts the tensions and toxins of modern life right off and lets you begin to be yourself again.
- Atchafalaya Autumn

A lone Cajun fisherman leaves the Bayou Benoit landing just after sunrise.

If we could live a thousand years, we would see, at Buffalo Cove for example, a phenomenal swamp with cypress giants growing exceptionally close together, towering, massive . . . unless they are destroyed by sediment . . . or cut for lumber in an overpopulated world more starved for wood products than ever . . . or killed by air pollution or acid rain. . . .
– Atchafalaya Autumn

(Far left) Dipping for shad from the wing wall of the Old River Control Structure. (Near left) A boatload of buffalofish caught using a hoopnet. (Bottom) Dipping shad at the Henderson Lake Control Structure, near Catahoula.

Catching shad and other "trash" fish is a source of income for many people in the Atchafalaya area. These fish are sold primarily to dealers who re-sell them to crawfishermen as bait fish. The cost of bait is the largest single expense for crawfishermen.

Shad are caught by dip-netting in turbulent waters, while fish of several species are caught with purse seines. Some crawfishermen catch their own bait—buffalofish and other types of carp—in hoopnets.

The essence of the good life in the Atchafalaya Basin a generation ago: Roy and Annie Blanchard share an early morning cup of coffee before beginning to check their fur animal traps along the Sibon Canal in St. Martin Parish – December 1980.

People of the Atchafalaya

Roy Blanchard   June 2006

Roy Blanchard was born in Catahoula in 1941. He has worked as a fisherman, moss picker, trapper and, since the early 1950s as a crawfishman, along with his wife and assistant, Annie. Water levels in the Basin were so low in 2000 that Roy went out to find a job, unable to earn any money crawfishing, and the same was true of hundreds of other fishermen. Some found jobs; some didn't. Roy began working as the maintenance man at Holiday Inn Express, on I-10 at the Henderson exit. When water conditions are right, he fishes for food every day after work, for catfish and for crabs.

Sport fishermen frequently steal his floating catfish lines, with the fish attached. He's catching lots of crabs now, but he can't sell them.

Roy:
    You can't buy a commercial license, and you have to have a license, to sell crabs. The legislature passed a law that if you don't have a crab license, you can't get one.

Greg:
What's the reasoning behind that?

Roy:
They said they were having too many commercial fishermen! Can you believe that?

You know, I've got a fair job; I make fair money, but a day feels like a week there. When I was in the Basin, a day passed so fast, you don't even notice it—when you're doing something you like and you're where you want to be. That's about as good a job as I can get, you know, where I'm at right now, but it's still not like the Basin, you know? Because I'm waiting for 2 o'clock. I can't wait to get away from there. When I was out in the Basin, 4 o'clock would come—I had to leave at 4 to go sell my catch and get ready for the next day, but I really didn't want to leave. The day had passed so fast I never realized what had happened, you know? That's how it is when you're where you supposed to be and doin' what you want to do. To me that's the most important thing in your life.

And still, they don't give us water— water is the blood of the Basin. Without water the Basin can't survive. And you can go at the landing [Bayou Benoit]. I go ride at the landing every afternoon on my 4-wheeler. I talk to everybody, sports fishermen and all. They not even catching nothing. And they won't catch nothing. Because this year

Roy and Annie checking and re-baiting a wooden slat trap for catching smaller catfish. Large catfish can't get into a trap like this one and are usually caught on lines or in hoopnets.

I'd love to live in the Basin again. It's part of me, you know. You can't explain it; it's a feeling you have. It's just like every evening I can go sit on my wharf back here, and every evening they have a different sunset. It's just beautiful. And I'm always thankful for that . . . . that I can be one of them out there to see that.

It's not going to last forever, this life . . . you know that. It's a shame 'cause it will never be back the same way. I guess people that don't live out here, they say "It's so boring out there. What do you find to do?" I say, "Well, I don't find one dull moment." You just have that love inside of the you for the Basin. That's the routine of your life. You learn to live that way. - Annie Blanchard, 1998

we didn't get no water—the water got polluted. All the game fish went back there, not that far in the swamp because there was not water, but they went and spawn, lay their eggs, and when they hatched, they couldn't survive. The water's polluted; it's purple almost. So all the game fish died.

People don't realize, it's not just the commercial fishermen that lose. It's everybody. The sports fishermen—they all cryin', "Where's the fish; where's the fish?" I tell 'em, "Man, we ain't gonna have no more fish. Ya'll gonna have to go with us and explain that we gotta have water."

The vegetation rots, the leaves, the water hyacinth, all that rots. It makes your water get bad. Well, if that don't flush out with high water, it just gets worse and worse. Nothin' can survive in there. Now the crawfish, they go down in the ground to the water table and they survive there, but they not surviving like they should. They don't grow. The few little crawfish I caught this year, they were about half-size. They can't get big in that bad water.

At one time they had twenty-six feet difference between the Mississippi and the Atchafalaya. Twenty-six feet, Greg. They could give us five feet of that in the Basin, you know.

People don't realize what the Basin does, especially for south Louisiana. Another thing: You see, like this year they didn't have hardly no deep-water crawfish. They still fishing the ponds right now (June 11, 2006). You never see that. They didn't want to stop. Watch next year. The ponds ain't goin' to produce at all, because they are over-fished and they didn't re-stock. Without crawfish from the Basin to provide stock, 75 percent of your ponds gonna die. You can put that in a book—you gotta stock with deep-water crawfish to have good quality next season.

Those big pond owners are getting rich. When the price is low, late in the season in the Basin, they buy these crawfish at those low prices. They're done bred, they're full of eggs. They're catching up their money a hundred times. Without that, Greg, without the Basin, in the long run, they not gonna have no craw-fish, and you can put that in a book. Somebody better wake up—the ponds, they all against the Basin. And that's their liveli-hood. They got to get their stocking crawfish from the Basin. If you take crawfish from another pond, it'll do for one or two years, but after that, they lose their quality. They stay small. So, they better wake up. Another two or three years like we had this season in the Basin, the crawfish ain't gonna be able to survive. If you don't get good water for them to grow and come back—look, between what we catch and what the Basin loses from bad water—I mean, one or two more years like that, you can forget the Basin. It'll kill the crawfish altogether, kill the crop. Right across the levee, in the Cocodrie Swamp, we catch crawfish in there once in a while, because of bad water. I realize that if there's none, there's none, but like this year, they could have given us some water for a little while, just to flush out the Basin. The last little rise, Greg, it came to eleven feet—it never got in the Red-eye Swamp. Even the beavers kept it dammed out. It's a mess.

As long as the water can flow, it's all right. If it can come through Bayou Eugene and go into the Red-Eye and then flow south through Buffalo Cove. If you get a big rise on the river and it can't get into the swamp through the natural bayous, it'll start pushing that swamp water back north. You've seen that; those crawfish stop running overnight. And they won't run again until it evens off and the water starts flowing back to the south. Then the crawfish, and the fish, they start running again.

All those pipeline levees need to be taken out. Bayou Eugene used to go all the way to Grevenburg and Buffalo Cove, but when they dug the Sibon Canal, that's when it started silting up. In 1972 we could go into Eugene from the Sibon. It wasn't sanded up. Two or three years later, they had a big sandbar there, you couldn't go either way into Eugene.

"As long as the water can flow, it's all right. . . . If you get a big rise on the river and it can't get into the swamp through the natural bayous . . . those crawfish stop running overnight."

Roy Blanchard and dog with large blue crabs on Lake Rond.

Bayou Benoit fisherman Roy Blanchard running crawfish traps in the Red-eye Swamp, about 1985. Like most craw-fishermen at that time, Roy made part of his living trapping, net fishing, and catching turtles and bullfrogs.

I go to the meetings: I tell'em that—They don't want to open that bayou. Bayou Eugene all the way to Grevenburg. You can explain and explain and show them how the water works. At first the sport fishermen didn't want that; it would put muddy water in Grevenburg, but that's their survival, muddy water. Look, we can't crawfish year-round. You can't sportfish year-round, in the Basin, I mean. Sometimes you gonna have muddy water almost everywhere. It's the way things are. But that muddy water, that moving water, that's what makes the Basin healthy. But they don't want to hear about that; they want clear water all the time. They want to fish all the time. You can't have it like that. You can fish, but you won't be catching fish—like right now. Until there's water, decent water, it's going to get worse and worse.

And we need to try to save the Basin, for south Louisiana, that's a big thing, the Basin, you know. A lot of people don't realize that—your best crawfish, your best fish, even hunting for ducks and deer. This winter it was so dry, the hunters let their dogs go to chase the deer; they never saw their dogs again until Christmas. The deer went so deep into the middle of the Basin, they never came out; they went in places that would usually be under water. You try to follow them and you'll sink up to your waist in the mud. The deer go out there and the dogs went after them, and nobody could go get 'em.

I mean, it's such a wonderful place; you know, they're gonna let it...I wish I could do something about it. You know, I preach, I preach, I preach. I never thought I'd be on a job, a steady job. I always thought I'd be crawfishing.

Greg:
Roy, you and Annie have two sons. Would they like to be crawfishermen if they could, or not?

Roy:
Aw, well I guess so, man! Lucky for them, the work they do is in the wild. They drive airboats and work with seismograph. But it's not like working for yourself, bein' you own boss, doin' what you want, you know?

We're gonna move out there one day. Annie's ready to go. That's when it's the best, ya know, when we're on the houseboat, barbecuing, there's a little breeze from the north, it's quiet, you don't see nobody.

As far as the Basin Plan goes, everybody that's making decisions about the Basin, they don't know nothin' about the Basin. They passing laws over there in Baton Rouge. Nobody knows what they passing the laws for. When they proposed that—they want us to put tags on every trap, and they don't want to let us fish at night—stuff like that. Loinest Bonin was there, and look, that man, you gotta put a crowbar in his mouth and twist it to get him to talk, you know, amongst people. He said, "I can't believe I'm doing that." He stood up and waved his hand. They said, "What's your name?" He said, "Loinest Bonin." "Well, what you got to say?" He said, "I don't know what's the reason ya'll want to make us tag the traps."

The speaker turned to the Wildlife and Fisheries: "What's the

Roy and Annie Blanchard running fur animal traps on Gay's Slough about 1980, when trapping was still a source of livelihood from December through February in the Basin. Note the stumps, which are the remains of bald cypress clearcut from the Basin about a hundred years earlier.

"That's when it's the best, ya know, when we're on the houseboat, barbecuing, there's a little breeze from the north, it's quiet, you don't see nobody."

reason for tagging the crawfish traps?" They don't exactly know. They turned around and asked the man who was pushing for that—he's not a crawfisherman! He runs a marina! You think that makes sense? They don't know what they are talking about, and they won't listen to the fishermen. I mean, we live there, we see it every day, year 'round. We understand what's happening. But they just won't listen. It's like they resent us, like they want to hurt the fishermen.

Most of the commercial fishermen are not well educated and in the world of today, you can't get by. Like me, I'm not educated but lucky I had a daddy that was a carpenter and he learned the hard way. But he taught me carpentry, plumbing, wiring, and a way of life, you know, how to survive—and, that's what I'm doing right now.

"Get you a plate, Greg. Let's eat some squirrel."

Roy and Annie Blanchard, 2006.

Sport fishing, an activity enjoyed by thousands of people of all ages, has always been popular in the Atchafalaya Basin, especially on early mornings in the summer and fall, when the water tends to be clear and fish are plentiful.

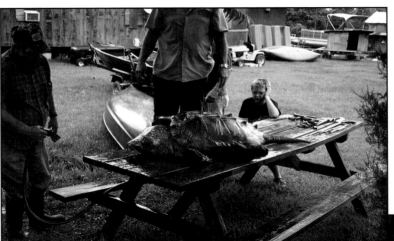

Blake Blanchard (below) enjoying the company of a 155-pound alligator snapping turtle's head near Lake Fausse Pointe State Park in Iberia Parish. A turtle this size would normally be more than one hundred years old. This one was caught by Cleve Bergeron on a catfish line near his home after it swallowed a hooked catfish. The meat of snapping turtles is a favorite of Cajuns everywhere.

Sometimes Cajun fishermen are able to find work as guides and advisers for film crews making documentaries, TV commercials, and feature films in the Atchafalaya. This crew was filming and recording sound at sunrise near Bayou Benoit – about 1998.

An oil drilling platform in the marshes of the lower Atchafalaya Basin south of Morgan City at sunrise.

Drilling companies still operate in the Atchafalaya Basin. This floating rig and quarter boat was searching for oil and gas on the east side of the Basin near Belle River – about 2001.

Dan Dugas running a gill net in a bed of water hyacinth at Lake Fausse Pointe. (At left) Dugas repairing a gill net near his home at Bayou Benoit.

(Opposite) White pelicans in shallow water near Henderson. Mature white pelicans have a wingspan of nine feet, making them the largest birds in the Basin.

(Above) Bernard Blanchard with an average catch of crawfish, about four pounds, in the Jackass Bay area. (At right) A below average catch in the same area several years later. Note the difference in the number of crawfish in each trap.

Catches have decreased regularly in the last twenty-five years. Only when the Mississippi and other rivers are supplying flood-level volumes of water to the Atchafalaya do the fishermen find a large enough population of crawfish to earn a valid livelihood. Recent good years for wild crawfishing were 1983, 1993, 1995, and 1997.

Crawfisherman Claude Broussard often catches his own bait—buffalofish, a species of carp. (At right) He lifts a hoopnet in the Cocodrie Swamp, Spring 2004. A lead net is attached to the mouth of this hoopnet, helping to lead fish into the cylindrical hoopnet.

(Below) Visitors from Washington, California, and Ireland observe Broussard and his son Matt, as they run a hoopnet in the Bayou Benoit area, March 2007.

My purpose is to reveal the beauty of the Atchafalaya Basin to people who have never seen it or who have seen it without looking carefully, in the hope that a great deal of interest might be generated to help keep the Basin as it is for everyone, including the hundreds of fishermen and trappers, most of them French-speaking Cajuns like myself, who depend on the area for their livelihoods. - Seasons of Light in the Atchafalaya Basin

The Atchafalaya may not be able to provide you with the kind of life and livelihood it's provided for me and my ancestors. When it comes time for you to inherit the Atchafalaya, it won't be the place I knew as a child, or even the place we know today. ~ The Land of Dead Giants

Sherbin Collette weighing a 63-pound yellow catfish and holding a 19-pounder, along with three of his grandchildren. Sherbin and his wife Louella fish together just about every day, either for catfish, crawfish, crabs, or shrimp, but their grandchildren will almost certainly never become commercial fishermen in spite of their natural interest in accompanying their grandparents, due to the constantly decreasing productivity of the Atchafalaya system as well as the coastal marshes ~ Henderson, about 1997.

A blue catfish in the hands of Sherbin Collette. Catfishing goes on all year long in and around the Basin.

This is about as big a catfish as can be sold locally. Fish the size of the 63-pounder (opposite page) are not sought after by the public, who are more likely to purchase filleted catfish of the size they would see in restaurants and supermarkets. For this reason, the catfish industry that once provided income for thousands of Cajun fishermen and others has been taken over by catfish farming operations, which produce a consistent supply of same-sized fish.

People of the Atchafalaya

Sherbin and Louella Collette   May 2006

Sherbin and his wife Louella are both about 57 years old, and they've fished commercially together since they were married about 40 years ago. They have two boys and one girl, none of whom live from fishing. Sherbin was elected mayor of the town of Henderson in 2004.

Sherbin:
There are almost no young crawfishermen today. A lot of them have more education now and I think they're smart enough to know that there's really truly no future in fishing. Now it's more of a part-time job than a full-time. When I grew up, the only thing I had in my mind was that I was going to be a commercial fisherman the rest of my life, and not do anything else. It's hard, I mean—how hard you have to work to make a living and keep your family secure. A lot of young ones thought it was easy and they found out that it's not. It's not easy living. Very, very few people can do it now. You can't raise a family on that. It's so inconsistent now. Usually, the crawfish season was our best thing. We always made enough to survive the year. Then you had your catfish and

your shrimp and crabs. It was a good life. Everything I own I owe to commercial fishing—no doubt about it.

My opinion of the Basin—if it continues like the last ten years, we might have ten or at the most twenty years left for commercial fishing. And that's sad. I do regret now that that's all I had in my head—to be a commercial fisherman. I hated school with a purple passion. To me, it took away fishing from me. Before daylight I'd go run lines. I'd come back, take a bath, go to school. Coming back in the afternoon, Daddy had my bait cut. I'd take off and go run crawfish traps in the afternoon. That's all I ever wanted to do. School was taking me away from fishing. I regret it now though. I could use that education that I missed. I graduated from high school, but there was no question what I wanted to do—no doubt at all.

Once Louella started fishing with me—well, we raised all our kids with commercial fishing. There's nothing on earth my two boys would prefer to do than fishing, and it took a long time for me to actually sink it in their heads that you cannot do it. Find you a job, do a little bit fishing part-time. It's in the blood. There's no doubt about it—it's in the blood. Even my grandkids, I can see those looks when we bring them with us.

Our only hope for the Basin is the federal money that's coming in. I say, let 'em spend it. Let 'em try to preserve the Basin as long as they can.

"I hated school with a purple passion. To me, it took away fishing from me."

Sometimes the catch is nearly too heavy to pull into a fisherman's boat. Sherbin Collette is fortunate to have the assistance of his son on this foggy morning on the West Borrowpit Canal in St. Martin Parish.

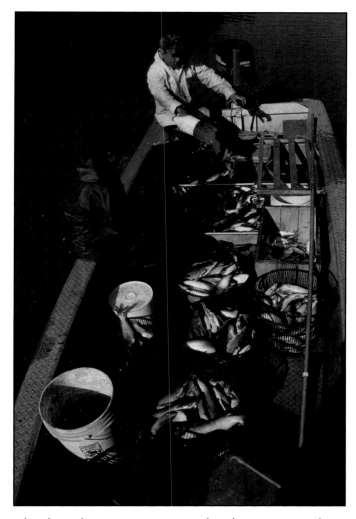

Sherbin throws water into his boat to wash it out while Louella looks on, their catch of ideal-sized catfish sorted into baskets of manageable size and weight. The wooden crate holds bait fish.

"That water is like blood that flows through our veins. Water is the lifeblood of the Basin. Without it, it'll die."

Now is the time. If something's not done, we don't have long in the Basin left. We need to open lots of old canals and bayous—re-establish that north-south flow—put fresh water throughout the Basin. That water is like blood that flows through our veins. Water is the lifeblood of the Basin. Without it, it'll die. And that's what's happening now. There's so much stagnant water all over. Swamps that my father brought me to when I was ten or twelve years old—swamps that I could see were so alive . . . now, they're dead. Nothing there . . . it's pitiful to see that.

And you know, if I saw it in my lifetime, my kids won't see it. It won't last for them—no way on earth. I still think there's things can be done. If the monies come in and they open the bayous and stuff. Siltation is still a big problem. The problems of the Basin are man-made. All the spoil banks they put along pipelines and location canals—whatever. Any restrictions [to water flow] hurt the Basin. It took many years to come to a point—to almost kill it. That's where it's at now. I haven't made a cent fishing this year. If I had to stop, I'd have to find a job, and you not going to find no easy job at 56 years old—Good-paying jobs, they got so many young kids coming out of college, they get the better jobs. Minimum wage would be tough for a guy like me that's 56 years old. Now I'm the mayor of Henderson—they're proposing a raise for me, which would help a hell of a lot.

Since Hurricane Katrina until right now—I have all my paperwork—in the catfish I didn't make a penny. I'm in the hole with that. Crawfish—I made very, very few dollars—that was in a pond, not deep water [the Atchafalaya Basin]. I didn't crawfish out there this season at all.

Its definitely possible I might have to do something else. What it would be I don't know. My sons fish with me on weekends, but they're working full time at Lafayette Marble and Tile, flooring, granite. Both of 'em working at the same place. It's not like commercial fishing. My two boys feel that pull to the Basin—no doubt about it. Just last year they asked me, "Daddy, you think we ought to take a leave from the job and go fish?" I said, "Absolutely not." One week after they asked me that question, all the crawfish where me and Louella were fishing all died—dead in the traps. That would have been a big mistake for them. We didn't hardly make nothing after that—why? Stagnant water in the Basin. You cannot depend on a season in the Basin anymore. Look at this year! You can be catching and in a week it's all gone. Everybody goes through that. Always, at some point in the season we'd scrape up enough to survive. This year, people can't do it. With the price of gas and the bait. I don't see how any fisherman can make anything. There's almost no crawfish.

Greg:
How do you feel about the fact that your chosen way of life is ending? Is it important to you as an individual?

Sherbin:
Definitely, definitely. You know, a lot of people moved out of the area to go to better paying jobs. I never did. I worked in the oilfields for five and a half years, but I couldn't leave fishing. In the afternoons—I was still fishing. One thing I can say—and I think I'm speaking for all the commercial fishermen—we all took it for granted that things were never going to change. This was our life forever. And you know, really and truly, and I did it myself, we'd throw our trash in the Basin, our bait boxes and stuff. It was going to rot or whatever. It took an outsider to point out to me what I was doing, a school teacher from St. Louis, made me realize that I was ruining the beauty of the Basin. From that point on, for the first time in my life, I actually saw the beauty of it—not just a swamp, and I love the swamp, but I wasn't seeing the beauty.

From then on, Louella and I, we ride in the sloughs and bayous and we'll say, "Just look at this place!" And I've been there all my life, but I never saw the beauty of it. You have to protect it. We're looking at something here, and we're losing it. And we're losing it at a fast rate. That's the saddest thing. Going in the Basin now, anyhow somebody's blind, that's fished all his life, he would know. You could put a blind person in a boat and go ride him in the swamp and he'll tell you the problem. Because he'll smell it. He'll smell that bad water, and he'll know. It's sickening to see that.

Preparing to raise a fish net near I-10, about 2004. The welded aluminum boat is the same one used for crabbing and crawfishing at different times of year.

"One thing I can say—and I think I'm speaking for all the commercial fishermen—we all took it for granted that things were never going to change. This was our life forever."

"Last year at Belle River it was terrific. Oh, Lord, oh man! They had good water going through there last year. Every year, the area where you can fish in good, moving water is getting smaller and smaller. The area where crawfish is actually caught is shrinking every year."

Sherbin and Louella Collette raising a catfish hoopnet in the shadow of the elevated Interstate-10 expressway – about 2004.

My boys, they don't hate what they're doing. But they don't love it like fishing. No way on earth. They love fishing. But the don't have that choice, not at all. There's no one kind of fishing you can depend on—catfishing, crawfishing, and shrimp. My boys shrimp on the weekend—they been catching a lot of crabs.

The Basin, once it's gone, it'll never come back. The fishermen nowadays, their kids are not fishing. In this generation it'll be gone, and it'll be in a short time. You not looking at a lot of years. To me the Basin in the last ten years deteriorated faster than in the thirty years prior to that. That's obvious. Last year at Belle River it was terrific. It was unbelievable the crawfish they caught. But it's inconsistent. I couldn't fish way over there last year, the first year I was mayor. There's no way I could do it. But I missed it. I'd hear about all they were catching. Oh, Lord, oh man! They had good water going through there last year. Every year, the area where you can fish in good, moving water is getting smaller and smaller. The area where crawfish is actually caught is shrinking every year.

I hope I can see the swamps come back to life in my lifetime. We'd better not miss the money from the federal government. We'll never see it again, if we do. They've got to spend it on water quality.

We don't necessarily need more water from the Mississippi. We need better circulation. Commercial fishermen always pray for water. But you got to watch your prayers. You can't pray that you get an amount that drowns people up North. That doesn't make any sense. Or drowns Morgan City. The depth of the water is not nearly as important as the flow—the north to south water flow. You don't need ten feet of water. Two or three feet of water, if there's a current, you're going to catch all the crawfish you want. The only reason we need high water now is to pass over all the spoil banks. Two days after the water goes on a stand, after it misses passing over the spoil banks, a hundred thousand pounds of crawfish are dead in the traps overnight.

Greg:
  I mentioned to Sherbin and Louella that when I began research on *Cajun Families of the Atchafalaya* in the '80s there were many husbands and wives fishing together in the Basin. Now there are almost none. We were able to come up with only two or three families other than themselves—another result of the advancing age of the fishing generation.

Louella:
  The [crawfish] season never lasts long enough now to let us be able to save us some money like we used to. We used to set traps out in November and keep on fishing throughout May and June. That was the time when we caught good—you could make a living. If you're on a job now, it doesn't pay to quit and try crawfishing. It doesn't last long enough.

"The [crawfish] season never lasts long enough now to let us be able to save us some money like we used to."

The Collettes share a beautiful and unusual life, fishing and crawfishing together on a daily basis. Sometimes they get by financially. Sometimes they don't.

I don't mean to sound pessimistic about the Atchafalaya Basin. In spite of my disappointment over the things that have happened there in the last 150 years, and even during my lifetime, it is the place where I feel most at home, where I find beauty, spiritual tranquility and true peace of mind. For me and for many others who have shared the Atchafalaya Basin experience, it's like no other place on earth.
- Atchafalaya Autumn

Sunrise in the Red-eye Swamp.

Sunset - Lake Fausse Pointe.

Roy Blanchard and grandson Justin feed a barred owl from the boat with a piece of shad or other crawfish bait - about 1997.

Barred owls are commonly sighted by visitors to the Atchafalaya Basin.

Children and Nature

Richard Louv, in his 2005 book, *Last Child in the Woods*, uses the term "Nature Deficit Disorder" to identify a condition that has become more and more apparent to me during the last decade. Children in developed countries just don't experience nature in the same ways or to the same extent that they did in years past, and this fact is becoming more and more evident in their physical and psychological health, as well as in their ability to develop and maintain a sense of wonder.

William Wordsworth wrote:

One impulse from a vernal wood
May teach more of man,
Of moral evil and of good,
Than all the sages can. . . .

There is an undeniable connection between children's outdoor activities and their overall wellbeing. Young people who spend hours each day sitting at electronic screens never experience intimacy with nature on any regular basis, and their health suffers. Earlier generations didn't have this problem. ". . . A growing body of evidence indicates that direct exposure to nature is essential for physical and emotional health." (Louv, p. 34)

A few years ago I did a slide/lecture program for a class of about thirty high school seniors in the small town of Loreauville. At one

A young hunter enjoys the thrill of a duck hunt near Crook Chene Cove. The Atchafalaya is an ideal place for children to bond with their elders, either in boating, hunting and fishing, canoeing, or camping.

The photographer's granddaughter Bridget Guirard and a friend riding a piece of cypress driftwood near Bayou Benoit - Summer 2006.

point I asked how many students had been into the Atchafalaya Basin by boat. I was surprised when only three hands went up. Then I asked how many had older relatives who had earned, or still earned, their livelihood in the Basin. Almost every hand went up. It didn't make sense. Loreauville is only eight or ten miles from the western edge of the Atchafalaya Basin. Of course, young people are not following their elders anymore into a life of fishing, alligator hunting, and crawfishing to earn a living, and this is unfortunate in many ways, but why is this generation of young people ignorant of the meaning and the beauty of that wonderful place?

A friend of mine conducted a sociological research project, about five years ago, into the lives of commercial fishing families in this area (St. Martin Parish). One of her interview questions was, "Do you have children?" Then, "How many of your children plan to fish or crawfish for a living?" All twenty families had children of various ages. Not one child planned to fish commercially. Answers varied among the children:

"I want to marry and have a family someday. You can't make a living fishing anymore."

"I want to build a house and have a better life than this. You can't do that crawfishing, not anymore."

"My mom and dad don't have a choice. They have to crawfish. They're not educated to do anything else."

Caleb Wilson proudly displaying his catch near Catahoula.

Children and Nature (cont.)

"It's a beautiful life, being your own boss, out there in the Basin, but you need more and more money to survive today. I can't make it out there. I don't think anybody can, unless they begin giving us more water."

There was a time, not long ago, when a high school graduate in this area had the option of going to college or trade school, finding work in construction, in the oil fields, or wherever, or going into fishing and crawfishing. That last option has disappeared under layers of sediment and lack of attention to water quality. It could be made to reappear.

The Atchafalaya is still a beautiful place, but its productivity has declined with each passing generation. A great deal could be done, if the people of Louisiana and our government officials were willing to work together. The Atchafalaya Basin could once again offer the option of a valid livelihood to young Cajuns and others. The last vestige of true Cajun culture could survive and prosper into the twenty-first century.

I can tell my grandchildren, "You should have seen the Atchafalaya when I was a boy," as my grandfather said to me. And they will say to their grandchildren, "You should have seen the Atchafalaya when I was young," but each time, with each passing generation, the reality of the Atchafalaya is an altered, diminished one. Where will it end? Nature is at our mercy. - Atchafalaya Autumn

Bridget Guirard admiring an American lotus at Lake Fausse Pointe.

The Atchafalaya Basin was, for a long time, a refuge from blind and omnivorous progress, an island of calm in a sea of hustle and confusion, an almost uninhabited wilderness, halfway between the population centers of Lafayette and Baton Rouge. Like Faulkner's ancient bear, it was "an anachronism indomitable and invincible out of an old dead time." A person who needed solitude and serenity could always find them in the Basin. It was beautiful, uncrowded and free.
- Seasons of Light in the Atchafalaya Basin

Sunrise with canoeists near Bayou Benoit - Fall 2001.

Is the Cajun fishing lifestyle as we know it today going to survive into the future as a viable, significant aspect of our culture and human environment—a vital and real part of our descendants' inheritance—or will it die out and become a memory of something irreplaceable that could have been saved by serious and active concern? Consciously or unconsciously, we are all making this decision today. Two or three years from now it will be too late. If we don't stop it today, the genuine will gradually fade into the artificial. Slowly the Cajun fishing culture will atrophy into nothing more than another roadside attraction—a subject to be studied in cultural history classes in colleges and universities rather than a viable lifestyle for thousands.

Very few Atchafalaya Basin fishermen still use live boxes to keep their fish fresh for market, but Connie Serrette still transfers fish from his boat to his live boxes until the market is ready to receive his catch. Having three live boxes allows Connie to separate his catfish from such other species as buffalofish, choupique, and gaspergou.

An osprey lands on its nest in the Cocodrie Swamp.

Having no rattle, the water moccasin, or cotton mouth, gives warning with the pure-white flash of the inside of its mouth, easily noticeable in the drab background it defends. Moccasins just emerging from hibernation like this one (notice shaded eye) are most dangerous since they can't see well and feel threatened by any sound or movement in their vicinity.

Red-eared slider turtles are a favorite food of Ozaire and Willis Bonin and the rest of their family. The Bonins have caught eighty-two turtles in their net.

Genevieve Arnaud and her son gathering baitfish for their catfish lines near Lake Fausse Pointe State Park – about 2001. Another income-producing activity of the Arnauds is to pick and sell blackberries from the vicinity of their home on the West levee.

Fire on the swamp, or so it appears. Actually, this is an unusually dramatic sunrise in the Cocodrie Swamp - St. Martin Parish.

A backyard crawfish boil always involves neighbors and friends. Cajuns enjoy catching the crawfish, taking them home, cooking them, and eating them fresh and spicy. The small boy in blue went hunting with his grandfather, Roy Blanchard, at the age of nine and killed a 350-pound wild boar.

116

A great egret taking flight in the Atchafalaya Basin. These white birds, with wing spans of about four and a half feet, are favorites of people visiting the Basin to admire its beauty and the wildlife.

Second growth cypress trees with leftover fishing gear in Buffalo Cove—
a perfect environment for wading birds such as egrets, herons, and ibis in late summer and fall.

Forty or fifty years ago it was only natural for a child in America to be able to experience the outdoors first-hand. A much larger percentage of the population was rural. In spite of that, we have grown up to be destructive and exploitive in our approach to nature. I suspect that the majority of children in America today experience nature primarily, if not exclusively, over the television or on some other kind of electronic screen. What will be the attitude of these people, as they reach adulthood, toward the world of trees and rivers, birds and animals, grasslands and deserts, swamps and marshes?
– Atchafalaya Autumn

Daughters of Ozaire and Ida Bonin, Bayou Portage, with the shell of a 135-pound alligator snapping turtle – about 1990. This shell was once used as a baby's cradle.

Nelson Bonin and Johnny Smith with a fairly good catch of needle-nosed and alligator garfish at the Bayou Benoit Landing - 2002.

Johnny Smith, Dan Dugas, and a young boy with an eight-foot-long alligator garfish weighing 252 pounds, at Bayou Benoit in St. Martin Parish. The fish was caught in a gillnet and processed for food - about 2001.

Father and sons—Jimmy Bourque with two sons, Junior and Kenneth, with an alligator garfish weighing 140 pounds - November 1985. About 10 years earlier, the family would have caught several garfish this size in one outing, rather than one.

Cajuns and "Making It"

Back in 1984 when CBS was making a film in the Atchafalaya Basin in connection with the World's Fair in New Orleans, Bill Geiss asked Roy Blanchard from Catahoula, "Tell me, Roy, what is a Cajun?" Roy didn't hesitate, didn't bother to explain that Cajuns had ancestry going back to Acadia, in Eastern Canada, (hence the term Acadian and finally Cajun) and further back to France in the seventeenth century. He replied simply, "A Cajun is a guy that's going to make it, no matter what."

After 1765, when most expelled Acadians began settling in South Louisiana, they came to be recognized as belonging to one of two main groups, the bayou and marsh Cajuns and the prairie Cajuns. Most of the prairie group who remained close to the land became rice farmers and cattle raisers. Most of the bayou group became small farmers, trappers, and fishermen. Cajuns have always had the reputation, both in Canada and in Louisiana, of being resourceful and hard-working people, and they have earned that reputation over and over.

The center of life and livelihood activity for the bayou Cajuns was, and still is, the Atchafalaya Basin. There are endless stories concerning what a paradise the Atchafalaya was in those days and how it remained a paradise-like environment far into the twentieth century. It was an area of unmatched abundance of birds and animals for hunting, enormously productive fishing grounds for everything from crabs and crawfish to turtles, bullfrogs, fin fish and alligators. The climate was mild and the soil was rich for small farms and for gardens. Most Cajuns grew and caught or killed just about everything they needed for subsistence living from the land the big woods and the waters.

Hunting, fishing, and trapping provided income for the purchase of those things that the bayou Cajuns couldn't produce on their own. Everyone had a milk cow or two, as well as pigs, chickens, and ducks for milk, meat, and eggs. It was a good life, in spite of the hard work it required.

After the Civil War ended in 1865, able-bodied Cajun men could get jobs with the land and lumber companies engaged in clear-cutting the big woods of the Atchafalaya and surrounding areas. Logging work ended around 1930, but it wasn't long before young men could find employment with oil drilling companies. Meanwhile, the environment remained productive, and fishing, trapping, and small farming went on as before.

Dewey Patin, his son Carol, and Fred Laviolette with 128-pound blue catfish - August 1986.

Wilmer Blanchard making a cypress paddle with hand tools.

A mother alligator usually builds her nest on a piece of ground next to the water so that she can be in the water most of the time but not far off, if she is needed to protect the incubating eggs.

After-school and weekend jobs for some young people in Catahoula and other Basin-side communities include working with the processors of alligators. Alligator season in Louisiana is usually the month of September. Farm-raised gators can be converted into meat and hides year-round.

A roseate spoonbill feeding in shallow water in the Cocodrie Swamp near Bayou Benoit. Wading birds like this are most common in late summer and in the fall when water levels in the Basin are the lowest.

A roseate spoonbill in early springtime beginning to build its nest in an Atchafalaya Basin rookery.

Sunrise with fog at Lake Fausse Pointe State Park.

Musician, carpenter, and fisherman Errol Verret with a 38-pound yellow catfish - July 1989. For many years Verret was accordionist with the famous Cajun band BeauSoleil.

(opposite) Roseate spoonbills feeding near Bayou Benoit during the low water of late summer.

Some older fishermen have never become crawfishers, staying with the practice of running hoopnets on the rivers and bayous. Kaiser Dupuis holds a 54-pound yellow catfish (at right) and washes his hoopnets at the Butte LaRose boat ramp on the old Atchafalaya River. Kaiser abandoned commercial fishing due to advancing age - about 2004.

The flower of an American lotus near sunset at Lake Fausse Pointe. Lotus are in bloom from late spring through summer. Unlike water hyacinth, lotus grow from roots attached to the lake bottom. Water hyacinth are free to float around with the currents.

Young bald cypress trees, part of our Atchafalaya inheritance, in the Cocodrie Swamp

Pirogue construction [...]
Patin's many skills—al[...]
hunting, and fishing—[...]
earn a livelihood in the At[...]
a century. Patin passed a[...]
2006 at the age of 98.

Legendary Dewey Patin, at age ninety, in a marine-plywood pirogue, after a morning hunting alligators. When cypress was available, virgin cypress, all pirogues were made of that material. Now they are constructed of aluminum, fiberglass, or marine plywood.

Three baby red-shouldered hawks in a nest in the Cocodrie Swamp near Bayou Benoit. While being observed these hawks were treated to insects and a small snake by their mother.

A member of Wildlife in Distress, a Lafayette, Louisiana, organization of caring people, releasing a red-tailed hawk near the Atchafalaya Basin in St. Martin Parish. Other species commonly rehabilitated and released include owls, bobcats, eagles, coyotes.

People of the Atchafalaya

Jerry Theriot - Catahoula   May 2006

When Jerry was in the third grade, his mother died, and he quit school to begin fishing with his father, Jean, and his uncles Condou, Marreau, and Tan Bourque.

Jerry:
We'd fish. We'd stay out at the camp in the Basin for five days. Then we'd come back. Saturday and Sunday we'd stay home, then we'd go back on Monday. We'd sell the fish to the boat that would pass at the camp. I'm 66 now, so that was in the late 1940s and 1950s. We did that until the bayous plugged up, about '55-'56. In the wintertime we'd trap. We'd do the same thing. We'd stay out there for a week. Then we'd come back home and sell our hides. My uncle Isaac Bourque would buy the hides. We made a living. Sometimes it was rough. Sometimes it was pretty good. I was just a kid. I had to furnish the meat. We'd go kill us some rabbits or grosbecs or anything to cook. Then we'd fish lines and hoopnets. They'd run the nets once a week, when the trading boat was ready to pass.

The fish we caught on lines, we'd keep that in a live well. If the boat was coming on Friday morning, they'd run their nets before the boat would get there. Then we'd sell everything together. Everybody in the camp would mark their fish before they put them in the live box. They'd cut a piece of fin off or whatever, so each one could recognize his fish. We had only one live box.

They had other people doing that on the river. Old man Vivis and his son; they was right at the mouth of Cocodrie, in a floating camp. They had ninety feet of water right there. But the sand started building up. Our camp was in a little slough near Bay Ha Ha, but one year we put it on the bank. Every year the water would take it, so we started putting it up on a set of four barrels to keep it above the water and the sand. Every year we had to put a new set of barrels. Finally we had put six sets of barrels, end to end. That's how much sand would build up in that place, where Bayou Cocodrie hit Lake Rond. After we had put six sets of barrels, (one on each corner of the houseboat), we were high enough so the water wouldn't come over the bank anymore.

The water would be in the swamp in the back and in Lake Rond in the front. That was a lot of sand. It wasn't until 1973, the highest water we ever had, before the water went over the place where we had the camp. In those days the bayous were deep and they would hold a lot of water. But now, if we get high water like in '73, the Basin can't hold it. It would go over the big levees. The bayous and rivers got too much sand. The whole Basin is way more shallow now than it used to be back then. There's too much sand filling it up all the time.

There's no young men making a living just in the swamp. They can't make it now. Even when we have a crawfish season, after that, what they're going to do? They don't have nothing to do. And this year we didn't even have a season. There was no water. Catfish, that's out. Trapping—they don't trap no more. In the '50s and '60s until the '80s we always had something to do. There were seasons for everything—crawfish, catfish, pick moss, trapping, turtles, and frogs, crabs. They wouldn't start putting their crawfish traps out until after fur-trapping season was over. Today, you can't make it—don't matter how hard you try.

In the early 1950s, we bought us a truck. When we didn't have much of a crawfish market, I used to take the pick-up truck and go around Parks. I'd unload the truck—nobody had money. I'd come back with chickens and ducks and vegetables. We'd trade every Friday. It was easy to catch crawfish in those days. Those big traps would fill up back then. In fifty traps, you could catch all you want. What

Jerry Theriot, Catahoula Lake.

"But now, if we get high water like in '73, the Basin can't hold it. It would go over the big levees. The bayous and rivers got too much sand. The whole Basin is way more shallow now than it used to be back then."

"They had crabs out there in those days. You'd tie a piece of meat to a string and throw it out from the bank. Then you'd pull them big crabs right out on the bank, three or four of 'em at a time."

Jerry Theriot with old houseboat.

happened? It all filled up with sand. And not enough water moving in the swamp. Unless the water comes up, the crawfish don't come out of the ground and begin to eat and grow. You could catch all you wanted right along the big levee.

Out there, we'd eat what we killed. We wouldn't kill more than the camp could eat. If they told me five ducks, I'd come back with five ducks. That was for dinner. Don't come back with enough ducks for supper. Go get something else. They didn't want the same thing. I was the food hunter. My uncle Marreau would cook. It was easy to kill rabbits along the river bank around those willow trees. We'd fry fish, make cornbread and biscuits, whatever.

Sometimes we'd fish on this side of the levee, outside the spillway, in Catahoula Lake, Lake Dauterive, Fausse Pointe. You went where the fish were running. We had one putt-putt boat on this side the levee and one on the other side. We'd walk everything over the levee, our food and bait and all. On the way back on Friday, we cross everything back to this side. We had two boats at the camp. My uncle would leave an extra boat out there then we used pirogues too, to run the lines and trap and hunt. It was a different kind of life from what you see now. It was fun, though. When it began to get rough making a living out there, I had to get a job. I'd fish on my days off. I still worked mostly in the Basin, on service crews, building board roads for drilling locations, whatever. I always stayed with fishing when I got my days off. I liked that. It was a good life. Another thing, you could go and hunt anywheres you want. Nobody thought it would ever come like this. We thought everything was going to stay like it was. But it changed fast.

I went out there a few years ago. I found where the camp had been, but it was all changed. Lake Rond—there was nothing no more. It's just a narrow thing, just a shallow bayou now. They had crabs out there in those days. You'd tie a piece of meat to a string and throw it out from the bank. Then you'd pull them big crabs right out on the bank, three or four of 'em at a time. Then you'd throw your bait out there and pull it in again. We'd catch those big river shrimp out there—there was lots of things to eat.

Bozo Verrett fishes year-round. But his kids won't be able to do the same as him. Of course, he dresses the catfish himself, him and Ollie. He's got all his equipment already, but a young man could never afford to pay what it takes to get started—the boat and motor, the nets, the crawfish traps, the scales and freezers. . . . Buying the equipment would set you so far back today, you'd never catch up, not the way the water is now in the Basin.

When I was a young boy living three miles from Catahoula Lake, things were significantly different. Roy Blanchard lived about a mile from my house, through the woods; and he and his friend Raymond Guidry would milk their family cows, then run their catfish lines in the lake, before going to elementary school, barefooted.

Now the trail through the woods is a highway, and young boys don't run catfish lines before going to school, much less milk the cows.
- Atchafalaya Autumn

(Above) Cattle round-up in the Atchafalaya Basin, where there are no fences or corrals, is an uncommon activity. (At left) A similar scene near Brasher City on the lower Basin from the October 20, 1866, issue of *Harper's Weekly*.

A few people still find and salvage old cypress "sinkers" from the Basin. These logs, cut as trees over the last two hundred years, lie almost perfectly preserved under water. They are of no use to anyone in that location, so bringing them up from the bottom and converting them into usable lumber is a good thing. Vernon Rebert with a 50-foot-long sinker at Lake Dauterive Landing – about 2003.

It seems almost inconceivable to me that all of the great cypress trees were cut down, without protest or opposition of any kind. There must have been someone, I keep thinking, with the sensitivity and awareness and wisdom to recognize the need to preserve some of those magnificent giants for their own time and for future generations; someone who would stand up and say, "Hey, you can cut some of the big trees, even most of them, but you can't cut down every last tree. I live on the earth, too. It's not yours to destroy." – Atchafalaya Autumn

The Love of Cypress

The Atchafalaya Basin was once one of the largest forests of virgin bald cypress in the world. Native Americans had used hundreds of trees to make dugout pirogues. Early settlers cut thousands of the trees—not the biggest ones, which were, in a practical sense, indestructible and too massive to handle for the construction of houses, barns, boats, water tanks, fence posts, roofing shingles.

But it was after the America Civil War, when the big Northern land and lumber companies came south to exploit the land for its resources, that the magical cypress forest began being converted into cutover swampland. Between 1865 and 1930, all of the cypress trees large enough to make lumber of any dimension were cut down. Many years, the yield of cypress exceeded one billion board feet. (A board foot of wood is one square foot, one inch thick). Finally, all the usable trees were gone; the big mills were shut down and the logging operations moved elsewhere. The Cajun loggers themselves went back to a livelihood based on fishing, hunting, trapping, moss picking and small farming. Even without its towering cypress trees, the Atchafalaya was a paradise, but things were changing.

The only virgin cypress left behind were hollow trees and lost or abandoned logs called sinkers. For many years after 1930 there was a local industry based on the recovery of these logs. The rarity and quality of this wood caused it to become more and more valuable. Today there

Errol Verret sawing a cypress sinker near Catahoula.

Finding, salvaging and sawing cypress sinkers can be a lucrative enterprise, but it is extremely hard work. The log above, in the process of being dug out of the ground, had lain there long enough for a 100-year-old cypress tree to grow on top of it.

The Love of Cypress (cont.)

is less of it than ever and it is more valuable than it has ever been. Most of the logs that sank will remain lost beneath the millions of tons of sediment that cover most of the Basin today.

I myself have gone searching for and salvaging ("resurrecting") as many of these logs as I can find, ever since the mid-1970s. I found one log 82 feet long and another 60 feet long.

For several years I sawed the logs into thick boards with a chainsaw and guide and carried them out of the Basin in my boat. One late October afternoon, sometime in the late 1970s, I had arrived at the Bayou Benoit Landing in St. Martin Parish, my welded aluminum flat boat loaded with beautiful old cypress boards. The sun was just setting over the West levee of the Atchafalaya Basin. I had the scene all to myself to enjoy after a hard day's work in the swamp, except for one very old man who had just come in from fishing for bass and sac-a-lait among the stumps of cypress forest that had once characterized the Basin.

The old fisherman tied his small boat and walked over to where I was, moving cypress from my boat to my pick-up truck. For a while he didn't say a word. Then he began passing his hand over the wood, touching the boards with his fingertips. His eyes were shining, whether with excitement or tears I couldn't tell.

Finally, in a voice more reverent than I can describe, and pure Cajun, he said, "Dat's dat old cypress!" I nodded and went on moving

The Love of Cypress (cont.)

the wood; it would soon be dark on the levee. "I hadn't seen nothin' like dat in forty years," he said. He watched me for a minute; then he spoke again, "Would you mind if I help you unload dose board?" I told him that I would welcome his assistance. He passed his hands over every piece, almost petting the wood, his eyes sparkling. When we finished, he walked away and began loading his boat on the trailer behind his old truck. I've always regretted not having thought to give him a piece of old cypress. Maybe I believed I would see him again. I never did, but whenever I find myself exhausted by struggling through the sand and mud to get to a log I want to "resurrect," I think of that old man and his love of cypress, and I become energized and determined; my work moves to a level of greater significance. Nothing in the natural world has more beauty and meaning for me than sinker cypress. There is no other wood like virgin baldcypress.

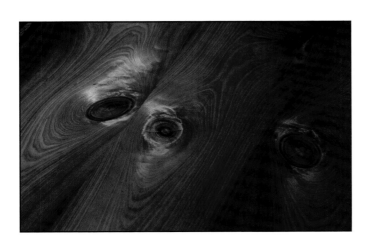

A calm, foggy morning, with a German film crew, at Lake Dauterive ~ Fall, 2006.

Claude Broussard, age seventy-seven, running gillnets in the Cocodrie Swamp near Bayou Benoit (left) and in Lake Dauterive (above) - Fall 2006.

"I started fishing in the Basin when I was fourteen, along with my dad and my six brothers. I love to fish. The Basin is my life; it means everything to me. I'm seventy-seven now, and I'm not going to quit fishing and crawfishing until old age stops me."

- Claude Broussard, 2007

(Above) Bernard and Roy Blanchard, first cousins, supplement their crawfishing incomes by occasionally guiding tours in the Atchafalaya Basin. Here, a group of students from Chatham College in Pittsburgh, with their professor, Sheryl St. Germain, gain an understanding of culture, environment, and water conditions in the Basin.

(At right) Larger operations, such as the one represented here on Henderson Lake, provide groups of tourists with a view and understanding of other areas of the Basin. Highway I-10 can be seen in the background.

Cajuns love a card game, especially outside on a beautiful day in the Basin. These four old friends are playing *bourré* near Butte LaRose. A marine plywood pirogue sits in the bayou at their feet.

(Left) In spite of the loss of the giant cypress trees, the cut-over swamps of the Atchafalaya maintain a level of beauty and tranquility that many Cajuns still find meaningful. These stumps and younger trees are located near the Sibon Canal in St. Martin Parish - November 1980. Sediment from the Mississippi River has made this area inaccessible by boat during low water stages.

(Below) Early morning in the Red-eye Swamp off the Sibon Canal in winter. When water levels are low, these areas can be accessed only by airboat.

It was only a few years ago, in the late '70s and early '80s that I could travel easily down the Sibon Canal at any time of the year. It was my favorite place to go when the river was low in the fall, and the swamps were almost dry. So much sediment has built up in the last fifteen years that the canal itself is dry from late summer through the fall. This is a great disappointment to me. There seems to be no way to prevent the accumulation of sediment in the Atchafalaya Spillway. Eventually the fishing grounds themselves, as well as their access channels, will disappear under many layers of sand and silt.
- Atchafalaya Autumn

People of the Atchafalaya

Ruel Seneca (with sons Gene and Ruel, Jr.)   June 2006

Ruel Seneca was born in 1931 in the Atchafalaya Basin. He still goes to his houseboat at Bayou Sorrel almost every week.

Ruel Seneca with sons Ruel, Jr., Gene, and Mark.

Ruel:

I was born and raised on Bayou Chene, went to school out there, through the seventh grade. We moved out of there in the late '40s. Everybody moved out gradually because we'd get high water every spring, get flooded out. I went into the service in 1952, when I was twenty years old. When I came out, got married, went to work, and I stayed away from Bayou Chene for . . . thirty years, I guess. When I retired I built me a camp out there and started going back. I mostly just fish for the fun of it now.

When I was a boy out there, I fished some, worked in timber, picked moss with my grandfather, my uncles. We had a barge, and we'd go down there on Crook Chene Cove, pick that moss all day long, eat boiled potatoes and salt meat. And they'd fish. They had trading boats that went from the Chene to William Talley's at Catahoula. Coming back they'd bring groceries, ice, whatever people needed. They had a store on the bank, and they'd supply it from the trading boats. Mr. Herman Larson, Mr. Percy Wisdom, they had trading boats.

The priest used to come out there, not every Sunday, but he'd stay with us when he came. There were very few Catholic families out there. Most of the people were not Cajun at Bayou Chene. You had Larson, Wisdom, Stockstill, Case, Curry—none of them was Cajun. We wasn't either.

I run fish lines out there now, just for my own needs, you know—go out there and relax. Just to be out there—it's good.

Greg:
I guess you knew Hugh Daspit and Dinkie. He was principal at Bayou Chene, and after they closed the school out there, Hugh Daspit became principal at Catahoula. He was my principal for the eight years I went to school there. They weren't Catholic, but Hugh's wife, Dinkie, was my godmother anyway.

Ruel:
It was a paradise out there. The floods got bad though—1927 was a real bad one. . . My old grandfather used to farm out there—cattle, hogs, chickens; he raised corn, sweet potatoes, many things—whatever we needed.

We used to walk to school. Soon as we got home, we'd hang our stuff on a fence post and go to work, wouldn't quit till dark.

You know Blackie Curry. He had that big hardware store in Franklin. They didn't leave the Chene till 1954. That's his daddy on the cover of that little book; he used to drive the school boat out there.

After the logging was over, most of the people out there fished for a living—turtles and frogs, alligators, crabs. When we wanted some crawfish, we'd tie a little piece of meat on a string at the end of a stick. We'd pass a net under that and scoop 'em up. Nobody was selling crawfish in them days. Nobody was buying. Froggin' was good. Deer? We didn't eat much venison.

Ruel Seneca being interviewed at Bayou Chene for a video documentary. (Photo courtesy Gene Seneca.)

Ruel Seneca, seated with son Gene, talking with Carrol Ashley.

"The Catholic Church at the Chene was across the bayou from the school and most of the houses. Every year after the flood, the Catholic women would go over and clean out the sand. They'd haul that stuff out in buckets until it was shiny clean. Next year it was the same thing all over."

For a long time there just wasn't much deer out there.

Maybe they didn't have enough dry land. They got a lot of dry land now. And a lot of deer hunters, too.

The Catholic Church at the Chene was across the bayou from the school and most of the houses. Every year after the flood, the Catholic women would go over and clean out the sand. They'd haul that stuff out in buckets until it was shiny clean. Next year it was the same thing all over.

Greg:
Well, you know, the highest water we had this year, at Butte LaRose, was 11.6 feet above sea level. That surely would not have flooded the church. Even the normal spring high water, the last few years, has gotten up to eighteen or nineteen feet, and still it's not enough to flush out the rotten swamp water and give us a good crawfish season. The last year we had enough water for a profitable season was 1997. It's been downhill ever since then. Some fishermen did well around Belle River in 2005. There was good water movement through that area, north to south.

Ruel:
Well, we always had water moving through the swamps and bayous in the old days. Any time of year the water was moving. We had a current through the woods back then. We don't have it no more. It takes moving water to give us a good crop of fish and crawfish.

Yeah, you could get by in them days. My uncle had an old dock made out of cottonwood logs, down at the bayou; he had one pecan tree not far from where we lived. He'd go out to that pecan tree with his .22 rifle if we felt like eating squirrels, come back with six or eight or whatever.

We'd go down to that dock to skin and wash the squirrel, you know, and them big blue-claw crabs would be trying to take 'em out of your hand. We could dip the skins, inside-out, in the water and get all the blue crabs and river shrimp you could want. Just shake 'em off in a five-gallon bucket and stick the skin back in the water and get some more. That was a paradise—while it lasted.

Uncle Billy would go and stand out there in that cold water with one or two shells and wait for them greenheads [mallards] to get all lined up. You could kill all you want with one or two shots. Usually that's all the shells we had anyway. That was back during the war—World War II—everything was rationed. There was nothing to waste. Now it takes 25 shells to kill your limit.

Gene Seneca:
They got a lot of crabs in the river this year. When the water is real low, at least they got crabs. They come up from the Gulf. By late summer, early fall, the crabs weigh a pound apiece. And they are full, and that meat is so sweet.

Greg:
What would ya'll eat out there, Mr. Ruel, besides crabs and fish and crawfish, squirrels, ducks and rabbits?

Ruel:
White beans and rice and gravy and bread. We didn't eat that much fish. Seems like it was against the law to eat fish if it wasn't on Friday. We sold most of the fish to the trading boats. But us Catholics couldn't eat meat on Fridays, you know. You'd never eat a catfish that was fourteen inches or more, that you could sell. The boats would take our fish to Catahoula about twice a week.

We didn't eat a lot of beef either. But we all had pigs. We ate a lot of pork. We'd butcher hogs every winter, you know.

Soon as they heard my uncle shooting squirrels, heard him from the house, a couple of his daughters would go out and dig some sweet potatoes. Squirrel gravy on rice, with sweet potatoes! That was good. Every time we fixed wild game, we'd have sweet potatoes.

There is a great deal of reverence today for what the Atchafalaya was many years ago, especially among those who once lived or worked there. The people (600 or more of them) who lived at Bayou Chene, in the center of the lower Basin, share the love of that place and its memories. All of them had to move away by the mid-1950s because diverted Mississippi River water would flood their homes and gardens, their schoolhouse and post office every spring. They and their descendants hold a reunion every September at a park near Morgan City to remember and celebrate what life was like out there, and every one of them who knew the place would go back to the paradise that was Bayou Chene, if that were possible.

The Seneca family lived for many years at Bayou Chene, among the live oaks that were eventually killed by river sediment. Ruel Seneca, Sr. still has a small camp there.

(Above) Ruel Seneca being filmed at a family grave at Bayou Chene. (Below) The Seneca family campboat. (Both photos courtesy Gene Seneca.)

Greg:
I was out at Alcide Verret's one day, on Bayou Sorrel, right at the river. It must have been 1983, because the river was rising so fast, Alcide was doing all he could to get his sweet potatoes out of the ground before the river covered his garden. I swear, we began helping him and the rows sloped and followed the line of the bank, you know. As we'd finish a row, the river would take it and we'd be on the next row. We got 'em all just as the river took the whole garden. I've never seen water rise that fast before. It must have come up a foot and a half in an hour.

We had crawfish that year [1983]! I was fishing half-time and catching 750 pounds a day. Big fishermen were coming in with 1400-1500 pounds. The processing plants couldn't handle it all. That's the difference good water makes.

Ruel:
I got some old pictures from the flood of 1927. They had boats tied up right to the front porch of the school house, you know. And that was a oak ridge all through there. But we had floods every year. We left there in about '49. We could have gone to Franklin on the west side of the Basin, or to Plaquemine on the east side. By the time we cast the houseboat off, we had decided to go to Plaquemine. We could have gone either way, just so it was away from Bayou Chene. We couldn't live with the floods.

Ruel, Jr.:
One day, right there at Bayou Sorrel, Addie Diamond Seneca, our grandmother, was rocking a baby on the front porch of the houseboat. She never realized that the rocker was creeping all the time, and it went overboard. My uncle saved Addie—she was seventeen years old—but the baby drowned. The reason she rocked off the houseboat is that she had her back to the edge of the porch, because women in those days—at least women raised the way they were raised—they didn't face the boat traffic with dresses on. So she dropped off the edge. The baby was Ernest Diamond's first child—he was just six months old. Ernest was one of eleven kids, all living out there on the Sorrel. That was back in the 1930s.

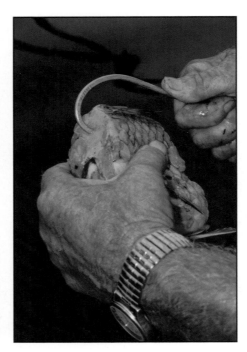

(Far left) Many foreign tourists visit the Atchafalaya Basin every year. from France. Here, Pierre Chatard helps harvest crawfish in the Cocodrie Swamp - Spring 2005.

(Left) Connie Serrette, Henderson, baiting a large hook for catching alligators. Bait is sometimes a piece of fish or chicken, a whole blackbird or anything else that might be available.

(Below) "Coon" Broussard with a large river crab - Grand Bayou in St. Martin Parish.

Autumn sunrise at Bayou Benoit.

Canoeing at sunrise in the Cocodrie Swamp.

(At right) His crawfishing skiff loaded with Spanish moss, Stanley Bourque, at the end of a day's work at Lake Fausse Pointe. Though almost no one else harvests Spanish moss today, there was a time, in the 1930s and '40s when South Louisiana exported over ten thousand tons of cured moss annually for use in upholstery in automobiles, airplanes, and furniture, as well as in mattresses and pillows. The moss industry died after the discovery of foam rubber and other synthetics.

(Below) A similar scene near Berwick Bay from the September 15, 1866, issue of *Harper's Weekly*.

(Opposite) Clyde Blanchard, near Bayou Benoit on a foggy fall morning.

(Top, left) An American alligator enters the water near Lake Fausse Pointe State Park. (Above) Great Egret near Catahoula. (Left) Diamond-backed watersnake (non-poisonous) begins to swallow its favorite prey, a small blue catfish, near Bayou Benoit.

For me it's like being terribly in love with someone who has changed and is changing in disturbing ways. Most of the beauty and spirit that I found so attractive in her years ago are still there, but some of her newer features are hard to deal with. If she continues to change, it is I who will be left alone, for I cannot bring myself to accept the transformation. I remember too well. I am too deeply rooted in the way we were. ~ Seasons of Light in the Atchafalaya Basin

A houseboat belonging to Roy Blanchard sat for many years on Gay's Slough near its intersection with the Sibon Canal.

illustration by Phil Seifert

LOUISIANA CRAWFISH PRODUCERS ASSOCIATION-WEST

Louisiana Crawfish Producers Assocation-West stands and works for public access to public waters, clean water, and public accountability by the local, state, and federal governments. We are the only locally-run, locally-based nonprofit group of the people working for a sustainable ecosystem in the Atchafalaya Basin. As former and current commercial fisherman, no one lives or depends upon a working fishery more than we do. As native Louisianans, no one lives to preserve our heritage—all of it—more than we do. As parents and grandparents, no one works harder to ensure that future generations can see and experience the waters our culture depended upon for a livelihood and a rich life of beauty, solitude, and sustenance.

The LCPA-West understands, as no one else, that the Atchafalaya Basin is a national treasure, but it is also the lifeblood of our culture. We will not stand by if individuals or agencies manipulate the Basin for the private gain of a few. We will not stand by if individuals of agencies work to destroy or incrementally chip away at our heritage and way of life.

The LCPA-West works for a time when the people of this state and this nation will see, as we so clearly see, that just as the heron and the osprey and the fish depend on a sustainable Atchafalaya Basin so too do we the people depend on the Basin for water, for food, for a living culture.

For more information on the
Louisiana Crawfish Producers Association-West,
please visit:

http://www.lcpa-west.com/main.html

Officers of the LCPA-West: (left to right) Mike Bienvenu, Alice Bienvenu, and Jody Meche.

People of the Atchafalaya

Jody Meche - Henderson, La.   May 2006

At 37 Jody is one of the youngest commercial fishermen he knows. He worked in the oilfields for about a year before buying his first crawfish skiff in the late '80s.

Jody Meche and his wife Tracy at their home in Breaux Bridge.

Jody:
I was brought up in a fishing family, so I tried to make a living running catfish lines and crawfishing. I learned that from my daddy. I just kind of grew into it; I guess that's what I was born to be. Fifteen years ago you could make good money crawfishing. In the off-season I would do construction work, electrical. When crawfish started up again, I would go back to that. I tried shrimping for a couple of years, but it was hard to make anything that way.

My two older brothers made the majority of their living fishing. I have two boys. The oldest is fifteen and the youngest one is nine. They come fishing with me and earn a little money. They enjoy it, but they don't see it as something they would do for a living. They see how I struggle with it and how everybody struggles with it.

If it were productive like it was 20 to 30 years ago, I wouldn't mind seeing them being commercial fishermen, because it's a beautiful life, being in the wild, being outdoors . . . I've seen so many things that other people never see. Working alone like that builds a lot of character and stability. It makes a stronger person. My wife used to fish with me.

It's a beautiful life, you know. I've met several men who fish with their wives.

I want to go on fishing, but you really have to work something else now to be able to take the time to fish. But it's getting so difficult to make anything fishing you really don't want to mess with it anymore. Right now I'd like to go and put me a run of traps (I'm skinning alligators now) but it's so expensive with the bait and the gas, and the water's real low. There's a lot of bad water all over the Basin. It's kind of hard to take a chance, spending money, hoping to make a few dollars fishing. I'd love to go, but it's hard to go when you come out in the hole.

As for the future, I don't see much of a future for fishing in the Basin, without some good projects that would restore water quality, make the natural bayous run like they used to, where they put the water into the swamp and through the swamp the way they supposed to, the water not having to jam up and back up and go rotten. I don't know if they ever going to do anything to fix that problem—I wish they would. They need to shave the spoil banks on pipeline canals so the water can flow through, north to south, the way it used to.

I don't think we need a whole lot more water; we just need the water we get [from the Mississippi and Red rivers] to be able to flow north to south the way it would if we didn't have the obstructions to water movement caused by the pipeline banks that mostly run east and west, sometimes for miles. Every natural bayou has been pretty much blocked off. We used to have a big sheet flow through all of the fishing grounds. The old timers talk about always having a current coming through. They had to put little weights in the cages sometimes to keep them on the bottom. You never see that anymore.

"Every year, when the river starts to rise . . . whatever I'm doing, I have a call—something calling me into that Basin, pulling me into the swamp."

It's important to me personally to be able to fish for a living. It's what I desire. Every year, when the river starts to rise and the rain and the snow melt starts—that river starts rising, whatever I'm doing, I have a call—something calling me into that Basin, pulling me into the swamp, but with the tough years we've had, you discourage that calling. You don't want to go and try it out anymore because it's taking a chance—it's not profitable anymore. I love to be in the Basin. If I could afford to be out there, that's where I'd be all the time, like my old man and my mom. They would spend 4 to 5 days every week out there, either fishing or trapping, raising a garden. That's how they survived all their life. No matter how much I love it, I can't do it anymore; we wouldn't make it—we couldn't survive like that.

Katie and Theodore Smith relaxing on their houseboat at Bayou Grand Guelle, in St. Martin Parish.

(Top, left) Husband and wife, Ida and Ozaire Bonin, fishing together at Buffalo Cove. (Top, right) Roy Savoy and his son Chuck raising crawfish traps in the Cocodrie Swamp. (Bottom, left) Jimmy Bourque and sons Kenneth and Junior have just landed a large alligator garfish in the Beau Bayou area of the Basin. (Bottom, right) Carol Patin and his son Dwayne bait a catfish line on the Whiskey Bay Pilot Channel ahead of a summer storm.

Ram Boudreaux running catfish lines from a marine plywood pirogue near Catahoula.

When my grandfather was a boy, the demise of the big woods had only recently begun in the Atchafalaya Basin. When he died in 1956, the process was virtually complete: All the big trees, save those that were already so ancient as to be hollow, had been removed. The great cypress forests had been transformed into cutover swampland.

Do I myself lack the awareness that would compel me to do something beneficial with respect to the earth that I'm not doing now, something that might be of vital importance to those who will live here many years from today? Maybe by the time my grandfather was a man of sufficient influence to attempt any such thing, it was already too late. By the end of the 1920s, the destruction was all but complete. Nobody cared enough or had the wisdom, or the vision, or the power to stop it. A million-acre cathedral had been converted into a million-acre graveyard— the land of dead giants— and hardly anyone noticed. - Atchafalaya Autumn

Sunset at Grand Avoille Cove.

I'm wondering whether this place will last. When my youngest son is my age, will he be able to find beauty and solitude here? Will he want to? Will the Atchafalaya Basin become a waste dump, with waters too polluted to produce edible seafood? Will it become so crowded that seekers of wilderness solitude have to look elsewhere?
~ Seasons of Light in the Atchafalaya Basin

Future Inheritance

There are many reasons why the Acadian ex-patriots eventually gravitated to the area we now call the Atchafalaya Basin, or Spillway, as it came to be known once the Corps of Engineers made a floodway of it in order to have a short and easy outlet for the high waters of springtime, to protect Baton Rouge and New Orleans and other areas downstream from the present control structures. In addition to small farming and the raising of livestock, as well as subsistence fishing and hunting, early inhabitants of the Basin could easily get work with logging companies if they wished, especially after the Civil War. Once the clear-cutting of cypress in the Atchafalaya Basin ended around 1930 large-scale employment for the "swampers," as the harvesters of timber were called, ended as well, and those who had profited from such employment returned, for the most part, to fishing and hunting, trapping and frogging. It was not an easy life in any imaginable sense, but the hard-working Cajuns seemed ideally suited to it, and, being independent and self-sufficient by character and tradition, they were able to be their own bosses, set their own hours, and live life more or less as they chose to live it—deliberately, as Henry David Thoreau might say. There seems little doubt that they had a real appreciation for the exotic character of their chosen environment. In *Cajun Families of the Atchafalaya*, I describe it in this way: "There is an unexplainable, almost mystical connection between the Cajun fisherman and the swamp, a desire not only to see but to touch, to be part of the wildness itself, to live deliberately in concert with the big woods. . . ."

Before long, still in the first half of the twentieth century, oil companies began exploration and drilling activities in many parts of the Atchafalaya Basin (about 1940). Many Cajuns, especially those who were young and able-bodied and who could speak English fairly well, began seeking and finding lucrative employment in the oil industry. The standard procedure was for a man to work for seven days on and be off for seven days. During his days off, he would go immediately back to fishing, trapping, hunting and eventually crawfishing, depending on the time of year and the level of water in the swamps and bayous of the Basin. It should be understood that crawfishing, not for food, but as a commercial venture, began only about 1950 in the Atchafalaya, and a few years later on crawfish "farms."

It cannot be denied that some families did well enough financially by combining their skills in working, fishing, hunting, and trapping. Those willing to work hard did fairly well. It was a good life, filled with healthy outdoor activity, good food, and, for the most part, lack of the kind of stress that plagues a more refined and "civilized" lifestyle.

But one by one the sources of income and livelihood for these hardy people disappeared: the big logging companies abandoned the area in the 1930s. Oil company activities have decreased year after year, and few Cajuns find employment there anymore. The harvesting and curing of Spanish moss, a year-round undertaking that once produced over 10,000 tons of black moss annually, has disappeared, almost all the uses of moss

having been replaced by foam rubber and other manufactured materials. Between 1875 and 1950, the production of cured (black) moss in Louisiana averaged about 6 thousand tons annually.

Catfishing, which once provided a major portion of a swampdweller's income, has diminished to a small fraction of its former importance. Most catfish are produced on farms in Arkansas and Mississippi as well as in Louisiana. Buyers and consumers value a consistent supply of same-sized fillets, the kind one finds in supermarkets and restaurants, and it has become almost impossible to sell a catfish weighing over five or six pounds, not to mention the previously-desirable fish that weigh in excess of twenty or thirty pounds. Most wild catfishing is now done by those few individuals who process their catch themselves and sell it from their homes. When they catch a really big catfish, one that would formally have brought a good price, they either eat it themselves or give it away to friends or family. The fact that these "wild" catfish are better tasting than farm-raised fish seems to interest very few consumers.

The same has happened with crawfish; crawfish farms now out-produce the Atchafalaya Basin by a large margin, especially in years when the winter and springtime water level in the Basin is not sufficiently high to allow the production of a normal volume of large crawfish. Only in years when

a large amount of flood-water is flushing out the swamps and bayous and providing the nutrients and oxygen found in moving currents, do Basin crawfishermen enjoy a catch sufficient to earn a livelihood.

Trapping has gone by the wayside also, for the most part. Comparatively few people wear furs today, and the mink, otters, raccoons, and nutria of the Atchafalaya Basin have enjoyed many years now of not having to worry about Cajun trappers. Even alligator hunters have seen a big decrease in the profitability of their hunting ventures. The month of September is normally the wild alligator season in Louisiana. When I was researching material for *Cajun Families of the Atchafalaya* in the 1980s, hunters were being paid over $50 per linear foot for their reptiles. Last season and for many seasons before that, the price had dropped drastically. This is because an abundance of farm-raised alligators has flooded the market and forced the price to fall.

So crawfishing is something of a last refuge for those French-speaking Cajuns who have always wanted to maintain their connection with the big woods and the waters, and who were typically not trained or educated for other forms of employment anyway. But crawfishing cannot be relied on anymore as a valid livelihood option. The children of the Cajun crawfishermen are not going to inherit a productive system of fishing grounds unless some major improvements in water quality and flow patterns are implemented.

What are the solutions to the problem of loss of productivity and livelihood-supporting fishing grounds? First is the control of sediment that enters the Atchafalaya Basin from the muddy Mississippi and clogs up the bayous and swamps with layer after layer of sand, silt, and clay. Second is the improvement of water quality throughout the system of swamps, rivers, and bayous. Only moving water contains enough oxygen and nutrients to maintain and allow the production of a sufficient crop of fish and crawfish. Only water that moves with a substantial velocity can carry its load of sediment out to the marshes at the mouth of the Atchafalaya River and do its part in restoring some of the coastal wetlands that have been disappearing for many years along the Gulf of Mexico in Louisiana.

Essentially, the Atchafalaya needs, if it is to survive as a healthy environment for commercial fishing and crawfishing as well as sport fishing, an increased supply of moving water from the Mississippi River and a decreased supply of sediment from that same source.

The pipeline spoil banks need to be leveled to the original elevation of the area to allow sheet flow north to south, and the natural bayous have to be dredged and reopened to their original size and depth in order to reestablish a healthy flow of current containing both nutrients and dissolved oxygen.

In May 2006 I attended a meeting of the LCPA-West (Louisiana Crawfish Producers-West Atchafalaya Basin) at Catahoula, an organization over 400 strong whose purpose is to find ways to help commercial deep-water crawfishermen make a living in the Atchafalaya, to restore the fishing grounds to their former productiveness and to protect the legal rights of all people to travel and engage in commerce on navigable waterways.

I proposed two meaningful questions to the fishermen in attendance:

1) How many of you have or had fathers, grandfathers, or uncles who earned their livelihood fishing in the Basin? – All hands went up.

2) How many of you have sons, grandsons, or nephews who are fishing or who plan to fish or crawfish for a living in the Atchafalaya Basin? – No hands went up.

My hope is that some effective solution can be found and put into action to improve water quality and water flow within the Atchafalaya Basin before this beautiful way of life passes from the face of the earth.

- Greg Guirard

Acknowledgements

Thanks to Malcolm Comeaux for his ground-breaking research on the Atchafalaya Basin and for the use of several of his images in this book. I am grateful to Edward Couvillier and Raymond Sedotal, as well as their families, for sharing their traditional boatbuilding knowledge with me and for allowing us to use several of their personal photographs.

Maida Owens, of the Louisiana Division of the Arts, Folklife Program, graciously allowed us to reprint here material on Atchafalaya boats and boatbuilders that is part of that organizations "Louisiana's Living Traditions" website.

– Ray Brassieur

I wish to thank Jerry Theriot; Jody Meche; Sherbin and LouElla Collette; Roy and Annie Blanchard; Gene, Mark, Ruel, Jr. and Ruel, Sr. Seneca; and Claude Broussard for allowing me to interview and photograph them extensively in the preparation of this book.

I thank Janet Faulk for typing and re-typing my text, Michelle Hebert and Cara Leverett for proofing and re-proofing every sentence.

And I wish to express my deep gratitude to all the fishermen and their wives and children who have allowed me to interrupt their fishing with my questions and my cameras since I first began recording their lives on film and on tape in the mid-1970s.

– Greg Guirard

Thanks are also extended to Phil Seifert for the use of his crawfish illustration and the Louisiana Crawfish Producers Association-West for their contributions to the book. For the use of their photographs we thank: Gene Senaca, Jim Delahoussaye, Philip Gould, the Louisiana State Library, the Louisiana State Museum, the Louisiana and Lower Mississippi Valley Collection at LSU, the Iberia Parish Library in New Iberia, and the Museum of the American Indian at the Smithsonian Institute.

We are also grateful to the Louisiana Department of Natural Resources, specifically Scott Angelle, Phyllis Darensbourg, Robert Benoit, Toni DeBossier, and Sandra Thompson for the use of their detailed maps of the Atchafalaya Basin (which were designed by John Snead and his colleagues at the Louisiana Geological Survey) and for DNR's overall support of this project. Lastly, thanks to all of the staff at the Center for Louisiana Studies for helping make this project a reality.

The Authors

Greg Guirard

was born in St. Martinville, La., and moved to the western edge of the Atchafalaya Basin at age two. Greg earned undergraduate and post-graduate degrees at Louisiana State University, but he has spent most of his life looking for his proper direction, having worked as an English instructor, a farmer and cattleman, a carpenter and furniture maker, a saw-mill worker, a crew-boat driver, a crawfisherman, and an actor/technical advisor to film production companies. He is most widely recognized for his photography and writing. Grge has self published five books: *Seasons of Light in the Atchafalaya Basin* (1983); *Cajun Families of the Atchafalaya* (1989, revised 1999); *The Land of Dead Giants* (1991, revised 2001); *Atchafalaya Autumn* (1995); and *PsychoTherapy for Cajuns* (2006).

photo by Drew Landry.

Ray Brassieur

is a cultural anthropologist with advanced degrees from Louisiana State University and the University of Missouri-Columbia, who specializes in the "folk cultures and culturally distinct lifeways" of the Atchafalaya Basin. Ray supervised exhibitions at the Folklife Pavilion the 1984 Louisiana World Exposition, Nicholls State University's Center for Traditional Louisiana Boat Building, and the U.S. National Park Service; as well as contributed writings to *The Louisiana Folklife Festival: Celebrating the Bicentennial of the Louisiana Purchase* (2003), *Raised to the Trade: Creole Building Arts of New Orleans* (2002), and *Louisiana Cultural Vistas* (Spring, 2000). From 1999-2001 Ray served as the Louisiana Regional Folklorist for the New Orleans region and is currently an Assistant Professor of Anthropology at the University of Louisiana at Lafayette.

photo by Greg Guirard.

For more information on publications from the Center for Louisiana Studies, please contact:

Center for Louisiana Studies
University of Louisiana at Lafayette
P.O. Box 40831
Lafayette, LA 70504
⚜
http://cls.louisiana.edu